# Success for the Diet Dropout

## *Proven Strategies for Women Who Want To Stop Hating Their Bodies*

Dr. Nikki Goldman Ph.D.

*Behavioral Consultants Press*
*Poway, California*

**Success for the Diet Dropout**



Published in the United States of America by

Behavioral Consultants Press
15708 Pomerado Road, #201
Poway, CA 92064
1-866-Dr-Nikki (1-866-376-4554)

ISBN: 0-9711350-0-2

Page composition by Silvercat®, San Diego, California

*printed in the United States of America*

# Contents

## Thank you

My husband Gene is sure I need a 12-step program for my writing compulsion. I thank him for bringing a sense of humor to my insanity. If not for him, I might really need 'Writers Anonymous'. I am a kite, and he is my string: always grounding me yet offering me plenty of room to fly freely.

My friend Andrea Barnes is always there to read my material. She makes me feel that I deserve the Pulitzer Prize, every possible writing award in the world, and a spot on the New York Times Best-Seller List all at the same time. Thanks for being my cheerleader She has taken good care of my web-site. I'm grateful to her for the good laughs which prevents me from sinking too deeply into my overly serious self. She takes me to the café when I need a good "let it all, out spill my guts out over coffee" and shows up at the gym on our exercise days to make me feel guilty if I don't.. She has kept me in all around good shape. I love you too Andrea.

My mother's willingness to have the bad side of herself exposed in this book allows me to be appreciate her wonderful loving side. While, as a child, I may have misinterpreted some of her words and intentions with a negative perspective, underneath it all, I know she has always loved me and wanted the best for me.

I thank my Dad for his ability to dream. He instilled in me the need to use my imagination. The ability to fantasize, put it on paper and make it a reality, has been one of the delights of my life.

I thank my children, Shanna and Jessie. I love feeling their joyful presence around me while I write. Their spirit of independence has allowed me to live my creative world and still feel like we are part of each other's lives.

# Foreword

We all know diets don't work. But few can tell us what does. Dr. Goldman's complete system approach to food, exercise, self-esteem and life will help you embrace a new lifestyle that makes you a winner. Never again will motivation be a problem. Finally, you will come home. Home to a place that makes it safe for you to be yourself. Bring your body and eating patterns as they are...You'll learn to carve away the 'fat of the matter' to bring out the real you and your natural body size.

A nutritionist was asked if any of the many diets on the market were any good. "If any of these were any good," he replied, "than there would be no need for the others." I lost a hundred pounds and have kept if off for many years. Had I known about Dr. Goldman's approach, I'm certain the weight would have come off more effortlessly. Nikki Goldman attacks the problem and takes a position no others in the field hold. She maintains that the secret lies in integrating body image and stress management into the process. Since diets cause stress and stress triggers the need to eat in an effort to reduce the discomfort of the anxiety, then diets can not be the answer. She suggests an approach that shows you how to deal with stress. Once you do this, you will automatically have a strong inclination to reduce excessive eating.

Most of us try to lose weight to get to a better body image. Since reading her book, I've learned that this is what has made the entire process so much of a struggle. Dr. Goldman says it's like going on a car trip when she was a kid. She remembers her impatience in wanting to get to her destination. Every few minutes she'd ask, "are we there yet? Are we there yet?" When she got a little older, she realized you never really get there because you're always here. Silly as that sounds, it is quite enlightening when you apply it to body image. If you feel terrible about your body, it's your outlook that has to be changed from within. If you're always looking ahead to when you will finally have the body that will make you magically okay, it will never "get there." Dr. Goldman shows you how to start with a positive role model for body image and integrate this all along the way. You'll learn to enjoy the ride as well as the destination.

This book is a pioneer effort. It puts weight problems in prospective and shows you how to carve a new pathway to success.

Dee Hakala
Founder of "New Face of Fitness" and
author of *Thin is Just a Four-letter Word*

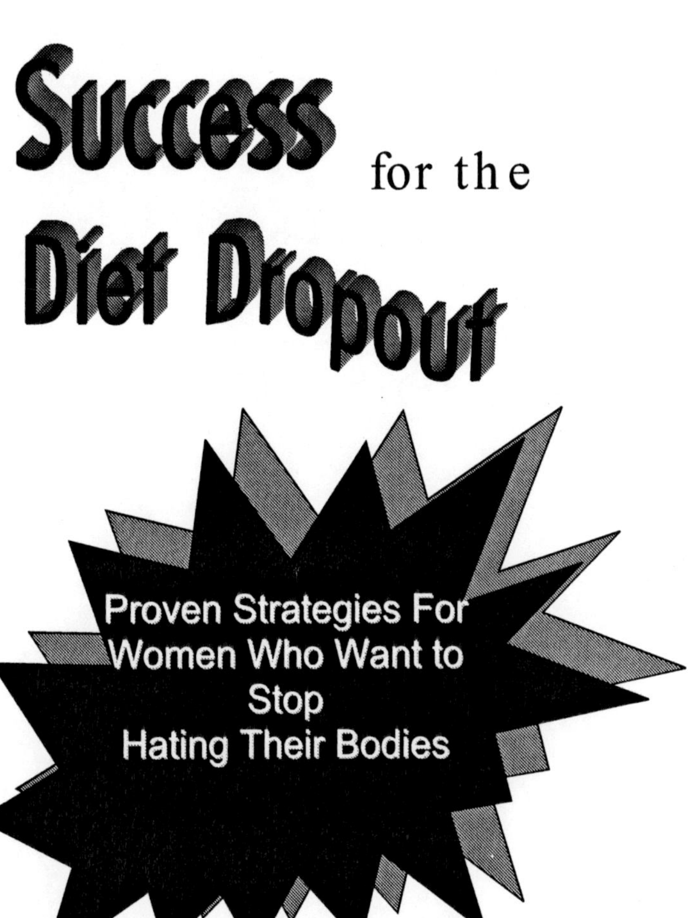


Dr. Nikki Goldman

*Food is not the issue; it is the symptom of the problem*

# Introduction

## *How to use this book*

You will find each chapter's concepts interwoven with stories of people who have used them successfully in their lives. Some are clients I've helped in my private practice as a therapist. Other stories illustrate ideas I've tried and learned for myself. At the end of the book are all the different recommended techniques, which will help you integrate the same ideas in your life.

The exercises are listed in the same order as they are discussed in the chapters. Feel free to go to the technique directly after you have read about each concept. Or you may wait until the end and do them.

However, to get the most out of this book, it is best to understand the concepts and do the exercises in the specific order they are written. You may be tempted to do the food exercises first. After all, isn't the reason for your interest in this book your desire to overcome your destructive eating patterns? Let me suggest that you resist. Otherwise, you will fall into the "diet mentality" trap. Food is not the issue; it is the symptom of the problem.

Self-esteem, body image, and understanding the role brain chemicals play in food choices need to be addressed first. It is only then that you will be armed with the tools to break the destructive patterns.

### *Building on a Weak Foundation*

Most people diet in search of better self-esteem and body image, happiness, and peace of mind. They go on strict diets and exercise rigorously until they exhaust themselves. This "all-or-nothing" destructive pattern does not work. It fails because they are building on a weak foundation:

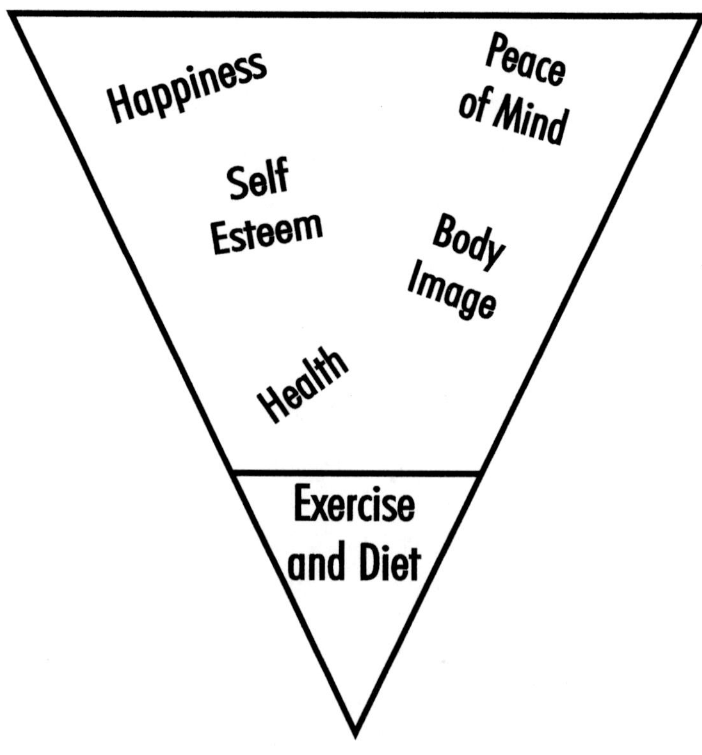

### *An Organic Approach*

Success for the Diet Dropout suggests a more organic approach: Work on self-esteem and body image, peace of mind and happiness in relationship to food and exercise. These solid building blocks offer sustained success.

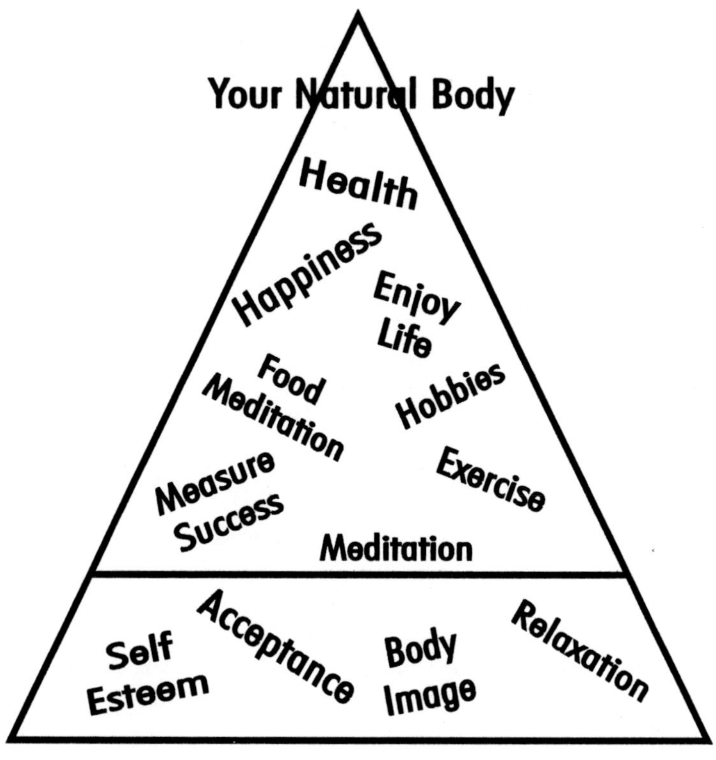


Surrounded by a world of body-size intolerance, I used to close my eyes and pretend I lived in a world that was blind. I actually believed that unless you had a certain look or a certain level of attractiveness, you could not be happy. Because I was fat, happiness evaded me. I'm not sure where I got this message, but it was a clear and distinct one. Then, one day in junior high school, I noticed a girl who was quite plain looking, and I spent some time observing her. I noticed a quality of contentment, peacefulness, and self-acceptance. She seemed quite happy to me. In fact, she seemed to have more happiness than many of the "popular" and pretty girls I knew. That image contradicted all that I'd been told up until then. I kept that image in the back of my mind and continued my search.

Reading a book like this as a younger person would have made my struggle to find acceptance much easier. Pushing me to lose weight became my family's noble quest. It seemed as though it was everyone's hobby, preoccupation, and their very breath of life. I will share how I came to be at peace with my body and myself and shed the shackles of my family's obsession with my size. I will talk about how I emerged from adolescence with my ego reasonably intact and how I continue to live an emotionally and physically healthy life today.

Are you tired of yet another diet to try and fail? Do you seek a refreshing approach to eating and body image that will get you back to natural eating and your natural size? This book proposes a complete system that teaches you how to reconnect with the wisdom of your body's need for nourishment, not the external dictates of a diet. It teaches you how to let your body find its own correct size, which may or may not be the size you wish and dream it would be. Most of all, it teaches how to accept your body—with its imperfections—and then embrace joyful living and peace of mind.

This is a strategy book, not a diet book. If you have been on diets, you probably know what to eat; you may even know almost enough to pass the dietitian licensing exam.

This book will show you how to approach the sustenance of life: food. It will show you how to shift the thinking process that sets you up for the same results—gaining more weight than you lost on the diet.

Insanity is doing the same thing over and over and expecting different results. This book is for those who are willing to give up their yo-yo diet pattern and try something completely different.

Is this book for you? Perhaps, perhaps not. It is far too sensible for the perpetual adolescent. An immature person wants things now and wants them delivered in her own way. Maturity means to accept life on life's terms, to accept the hand that you've been dealt, and to play those cards as best you can. Maturity allows your childhood dreams to evolve and mature into something that works for you in adulthood.

So even if you don't accomplish your childhood dream of becoming a famous actress, you certainly can enjoy being the best actress you can be. And that growth, keeps you from becoming stuck in a fantasy that insists you be the "star," the "best," or attain that ever-elusive slim body.

This book is for the intelligent person who has finally faced the reality that no individual's body is perfect. Keeping weight off involves a perpetual diet—and even then, the chances are slim. (My apologies for using the "s" word!) Ninety-five percent of all people who lose weight gain it back. So do you continue to gain at a losing game, or do you create a new game, a game that says you can still find beauty at your natural size? Once you do, you can get on with a life of value, a life in which you make useful and fulfilling contributions to others rather than being obsessed about the imperfections in your body.

To focus on yourself and your body takes a great deal of time; it is a life of self-absorption; not a very fulfilling life purpose. Nor does it offer much pleasure. The intent of this book is to reach people whose pursuit of a false dream has prevented them from living the good life and manifesting all that they are meant to be.

### *The American Nightmare*

People are literally killing themselves trying to be skinny. Obsessions for perfect size have driven many to use dangerous drugs. Others face the shame and humiliation of constant failure when a diet doesn't work.

Statistics show that 65 percent of Americans go on a diet each year. More than half of those diets last only 30 days. Nearly 70 percent of American women; and 53 percent of American men; think they should lose weight, but many are getting tired of chasing the illusive ideal image. Their futile attempts to compete, with the perfect body specimens portrayed in magazines, leave them at a loss as to what more to do. They desperately want something else. Although they want to stop the on-and-off diet insanity, most do not know how.

This book shows how to have fitness and good self-esteem at the size that's right for you, and then how to get on with the pleasures of life and peace of mind.

The ideas and techniques in this book can germinate healthy attitudes and behaviors so that you too, can find the peace that I have found.

### *Take This Quiz*

How much time and energy do you spend on food and body obsessions? To find out, take this quiz. (Later, you will be asked to take the same quiz, which will help to show the positive changes you're making.)

The goal of this book is to help you lose your preoccupation with your body and food and lose the idealized image that continues to sabotage your efforts to be slim. As you close that destructive door, I offer you a new one to open. I hope to help you integrate a healthy lifestyle in terms of physical activity and emotional outlook. In addition, I hope to help you reach a balance between paying appropriate attention to yourself and letting go of exhaustive and indulgent self-concern—and in so doing, get on with living.

**Instructions:**
On a scale of 1 to 10,
with 1 = "Rarely" and 10 = "Very often"...
How often do you:

### Body Image

1. Spend time thinking about what's wrong with your body or wishing you were thin?
2. Put off doing enjoyable activities until you "lose weight?"
3. Avoid sports, exercise, or going to the beach because of your appearance?
4. Compare yourself with others to see if they are heavier than you?

5. Find it difficult to enjoy activities because you are self-conscious about your physical appearance?
6. Think negative and self-critical thoughts about your body and physical appearance?
7. Allow guilt feelings or feeling bad about your body to preoccupy your thinking?

## Preoccupation with Food

8. Experience thoughts about food?
9. Have food thoughts that interfere with your ability to concentrate on a task?
10. Eat when you're not hungry?
11. Use food to comfort yourself?
12. Promise to go on a diet and find you can't stick to it?
13. Eat little around others and then overeat when you're alone?
14. Eat to cope with boredom?
15. Eat more when under pressure?
16. Find it difficult to resist getting something to eat when you're not hungry and others are eating?

17. Find it difficult to resist food when you're not hungry at parties and celebrations that involve food?
18. Find it difficult to enjoy food whether alone or with others?
19. Feel guilty about eating anything?

# *Upon completion of this book, take the test again, and compare your score.*

***My Story and Why This Book***

In a world that respects skinny...In a world that demands skinny... In a world that says you're nothing unless you're skinny, how do Camryn Manheim, Rosie O'Donnell, Delta Burke, and other public personalities manage to succeed despite their size? Attitudes are changing.

NPD Group, a consumer-marketing research firm, shows a shift in opinion about people considered to be overweight. In one survey, 55% said they thought being overweight was unattractive. Nine years later only 36% of the people felt that way.

Major influencing institutions such as Nike support these new attitudes. Recently, Dee Hakala, a woman who weighs more than 200 pounds, won the Nike Fitness Innovation Award for her international program called "New Face of Fitness." Her program shows women how to get fit regardless of their size. This is an innovation whose time has come.

I'm not a television star, yet I learned to succeed despite a world full of pressure to conform to an unrealistic standard. Although these demands made me miserable at times, living large through my journey of life, has been a departure from the typical scenario; diet, lose weight, gain it all back plus more, and feel worse than ever. I realize now my approach toward my "perfectly imperfect body" has left me perhaps a little less wounded than those who got on the merry-go-round of dieting time and again. And yet, I experienced a great deal of emotional pain too.

I remember my mother's useless attempts to get me to diet as a teenager. In fact, trying to change my body size by dieting had the opposite effect—I gained weight.

I must have had a sixth sense about things, because I somehow knew even then that dieting was futile. Often times, I wished I had been blessed with a slimmer body. However, after several failed attempts at dieting, I made peace as best I could with what I had been given. After all, the ancient Asian practice of bandaging woman's feet to keep them small and delicate is today considered cruel and oppressive. Why then should it be acceptable to expect large-sized women to squeeze themselves into slimmer bodies?

I am slimmer as an adult than when I was 18. While I am far from the ideal recommended by the weight charts, I am not nearly as large as I might be if I had insisted on struggling for that elusive perfectly sized body. I know a woman who dieted herself up from a size 18 to a size 24. Each time she dieted, she gained more weight than she lost. My attitude has saved me from this type of failure. I am pleased to have been spared the dissatisfaction and despair.

Through my personal experiences and the techniques I have developed in my private practice as a therapist, I offer these suggestions to those who want to liberate themselves from this oppression.

As part of making peace with my body, I worked on my negative attitude. I experimented with things that worked. I noticed that if I ate what I wanted without feeling guilt or shame, I ate less and was satisfied for longer periods. What a wonderful difference from dieting! In the past, immediately following the food restriction of a diet, I experienced an overwhelming need to eat excessive amounts of food.

In nature, every action has an equal and opposite reaction. The velocity of the upward climb of a rocket corresponds to its downward push against the earth. As an experiment, take a beach ball, push it down into the water, and let it go. Watch it rise above the water as high as it was pushed under. Yet people are astonished and feel guilty when a binge follows a period of severe food restriction. It's almost impossible for it not to happen. You cannot fight the law of physics. Well you can... but you'll lose! (Or should I say, gain?).

> ***In nature, every action has an equal and opposite reaction. The velocity of the upward climb of a rocket corresponds to the downward push. Yet people are astonished and feel guilty when a binge follows a period of severe food restriction. You can't fight the laws of physics.***

I discovered how to relax before eating. This made the meal more easily digestible and more filling. Gentle exercise such as a walk reduced my hunger. I began to integrate simple and enjoyable body movement into my day-to-day life. When friends quit their rigorous exercise plans because they had exhausted themselves, I learned how to pace myself. When I went through periods of inactivity, instead of forcing myself back to a dreaded routine, like my friends who played the "all-or-nothing game," I gently reminded myself of the pleasures of physical activity. I became easily motivated because I was enticing myself, not "force feeding." I actually began to miss exercise. It no longer became something I had to convince myself to do. I became internally motivated toward it. Even today, I go through periods of inactivity. But those times are less frequent. Exercise is part of my day-to-day life, not something I do for a few months during times of dieting and then recuperate from for the next year and a half.

When I was about 13, I met someone from South Africa. She told me about a special whitening cream that black South Africans use to make their skin lighter. How odd, I thought, to be living with Americans who spend endless hours in the sun trying to make their skin darker when others strive for whiteness. At that time, it was also in vogue to straighten curly hair. Yet others saved their hard-earned baby-sitting money so they could get their hair styled with a permanent curl. I realized my own dissatisfaction with my body was just as crazy. I wondered if part of human nature was to want to be what you are not.

Throughout the book, I will give you reasons to change your "diet mentality." I will offer supporting scientific evidence why dieting and the accompanying worry and stress cause more health problems than they solve. In fact, research at Yale University shows a link between chronic stress and excess abdominal fat storage.

I will show you an alternative lifestyle that will bring you peace of mind. It probably won't make you skinny, but it will likely get you to a more natural size with a healthy body and mind. If you've picked up this book, you are probably somewhat open to something different; yet you will more than likely feel a bit of resistance to the ideas.

The path of self-acceptance is not for everyone. It takes a certain independence. The courage to be different does not come easily. Some people believe that they will never change if they accept themselves as they really are. Nothing could be further from the truth. When you surrender to things as they are instead of fighting them, you build from a position of strength. Self-hatred only makes you weak. Just like a tree's dying branches drain it of the energy to thrive and survive, so too will the negativity of rejecting your body sap you of your vitality. When others tell you that you should lose weight, it is difficult to stand tall and say, "I'm working on making my body healthy and strong. My body will find its natural size." Yet, if you gather the courage to confront the prejudice, it can fill you with a sense of pride. And isn't feeling proud part of the reason so many people chase the rainbow of slimness anyway?

> ***Like a trees dying branches, drain it of the energy to thrive and survive, so too will the negativity of rejecting your body, sap you of your vitality.***

Before he died, a wise man named Rabbi Zusya said, "In the world to come I shall not be asked, Why, were you not Moses? I shall be asked, Why, were you not Zusya?"

In the same vein, most people approach dieting as if they were trying to become someone else—someone more acceptable. How then can we shift the focus? How can we make strong healthy decisions about our bodies, in an effort to become more of who we already are?

I remember seeing a chart that helped determine what type of clothes to buy. It showed the various types of flaws a woman's body could have. If you were short-waisted, the chart recommended one style; if you had big hips, it suggested a different fashion design. This mind-set starts with the premise that you are an ugly duckling. Supposing, instead, you viewed yourself as the swan. The question then becomes what fashion will bring out what you have?

For example, I was always told that I was short-waisted. As a result, I always felt bad about the way clothes made me look. Then one day I realized, if I was short-waisted, that must mean that I carry my 5'5" height somewhere else. Most of my height then was in my legs-not a bad thing after all! I began to stand taller and carry myself with more confidence. My whole body took on a slimmer appearance than when I was slouching from poor self-esteem. I automatically looked like I lost 10 pounds—the easiest weight I'd ever shed.

Today I believe that my body, in part, is programmed for a certain size. If I threaten to go below this, every healthy cell in my body fights for survival. (Don't despair at this reality; these limitations can work *for* you, not against you.)

As Rabbi Zusya suggests, be more yourself. Like spreading wildflower seeds, I'm sharing the techniques in this book so that you too can develop healthy attitudes.

### *It's Not a Single Issue*

Obesity is a baffling phenomenon. Psychologists discuss the problem as an emotional one. Nutritionists offer answers through diet. Do scientists have the answer? Is physiology an element? What about the hereditary factor? Does the set-point theory solve the dilemma? While specialists debate about the solution, Americans sink deeper into the quicksand of diets, more fat, and failure. Is it perhaps a problem of perception?

Homosexuality used to be considered a psychological problem. Now it is considered just another viable state of being. Approximately ten percent of the population is homosexual. And while it is not "usual" for most people, it is "usual" for this ten percent. Sociologists have discovered tribes who make a place within their society for homosexuals. There, they have a role as valuable as anyone else's. Is it possible that large-sized people too might have a place without ridicule?

Intelligence is another analogy. There is a range of intelligence from below average to above average and genius. Aren't geniuses simply an extreme of the norm? It is not normal for most people to be geniuses. However, it is normal for that small percentage of the population to be at the far end of the spectrum. Can it be possible that size works in much the same way?

Have you ever known slim people who eat quite a bit for their size and yet don't gain weight? Other slim people are small eaters. So can it also be true that in large-sized people both eating types exist? Is it then possible that some of us were made to be slim and others large? Doesn't it seem reasonable that if some slim people maintain their weight by eating smaller amounts and some don't have to watch what they are eating, then the same can be true for people of all sizes?

You will find techniques here to address both sides of the issue. If eating compulsively or emotionally is an issue for you then you'll learn to deal with it, with the help of the recommended techniques. If not, skip that part. Learn to accept your eating style and deal with the self-esteem issues that have made you feel bad about eating.

Consider the case of a teenage boy, self-conscious about tripping over his own feet when asking a girl out. He inevitably falls on his face. His fear created the reality. The same is true with fear of becoming fat. The very fear of fat can create it. Whatever you resist persists. It is a law of nature. If you resist fat, you will have to fight fat.

In an effort to resist being fat, most charge ahead toward rigid diets and rigorous exercise. This approach lacks something. For one thing, it doesn't work. For another thing, even those who get to their goal weight and manage to stay there for a period of time still feel their bodies somehow don't measure up. So self image must be a big part of the puzzle.

*Success for the Diet Dropout* is a complete system. It teaches you how to reconnect with the wisdom of your body's need for nourishment, instead of the external dictates of a diet. It will teach you how to let your body find its own correct size. It will teach you how to accept your body with its imperfections and then get on with joyful living and peace of mind. This system helps you leave behind the obsessions about food and body size. You will find a comfortable place for yourself in the world where previously you found only criticism and rejection from yourself and others.

# *The Golden Braid*

*Get a Life*

* * *

*A Body Image Makeover*

* * *

*Dare to Stop Dieting*

***

*Food: It's Neither Your Friend nor Your Enemy*

* * *

*Accept Your Body's Limitations*

*(Stop the Fear of Fat)*

* * *

*Measure Successful Behavior*

* * *

*A Place for Pleasure*

## Chapter 1

# Self-Esteem

## *What You Think Of Me Is None Of My Business*

*Why is it we judge ourselves by our ideals and others by their acts?*

– Zig Ziglar
Author and Motivational Speaker

A seemingly trite experience made a profound shift in my negative attitude toward myself. I was about 12 or 13 years old and was watching the TV show Bonanza. Pa and Hoss were together fixing the north fence, when Hoss expressed jealousy toward his brother, Little Joe. In a relaxed, matter-of-fact manner, Pa turned to Hoss and said, "It gets to a point in your life when you've got to make peace with who you are." A wave of awareness shot through me. Pa was telling his son that it was okay for him to accept and like himself. I felt an immediate affinity for this philosophy and took the ball and ran with it. With a deep sigh of relief, a life-long burden disappeared in an instant.

For many women, their appearance is the only basis for their self-esteem. Women are conditioned for this and pass it along from one generation to the next. My mother was no exception.

Weight was the main focus around our house. I knew on some level, my mother was trying to save me from the fate of criticism and rejection from the world around. She had suffered emotional scars having grown up overweight and wanted to spare me the same pain. Unfortunately, her attempt at protection backfired.

My mother had been confronted by her mother and older sister about food and weight. As a result, her daily discussion with me consisted of what I was eating; how much I was eating; whether what I was eating was fattening; whether I should be eating or not eating something; what effect it would have on my body; what I looked like; whether boys would like me if I were fat; ad nauseum. I often felt trapped as though I were under a microscope, constantly being observed.

This conveyed the message that my body will give me self-esteem, when and if it reaches the acceptable standard; and nothing else I do or accomplish will compensate for not having the right body. Therefore, I could never expect to have good self-esteem.

*I felt as if I were invisible on some level, merely a "walking body." Nothing about me was worth noticing except my unacceptable body and my equally undesirable eating.*

I felt as if I were invisible on some level, merely a "walking body." Nothing about me was worth noticing except my unacceptable body and my equally undesirable eating. My head even echoed from feeling so empty inside. In my twenties, when I lived on my own, I knew I had to change the way I related to my family. I wanted to have them talk with me as a total person with interests and ideas that had nothing to do with my body.

I decided to downplay the topic of weight and food. Each time I went to visit, my mother or my aunt commented on whether I had gained or lost weight. Although their observations of my reduced size were supposed to be compliments, they diminished my importance as a whole person because only my body was important enough to talk about.

Therefore, for several years, when either my aunt or mother mentioned my looks, I replied as if it were a non-issue. If they said I lost weight, I would shrug my shoulders and nonchalantly say, "Maybe I have. I don't know," and then change the subject. If they'd say I gained weight, I responded in the exact same way.

They might just as well have asked if I thought it were going to rain that day. Because they got little emotional response from me. Eventually they stopped making my body the main focus. This was quite freeing. It took several years to accomplish, but the effort paid off. I was finally able to visit without the negative anticipation of whether I looked good enough. However, I must say, for years after they stopped talking to me about my body, it seemed as though they were making the judgments in silence. Out of the corner of my eye, I would notice them looking me over. I had trained them not to mention their

> ***It wasn't until years later that I felt as though they too had overcome their destructive obsessions.***

criticisms to me; yet they couldn't help their unhealthy preoccupation within themselves. Not until years later did I feel as though they too had overcome their destructive obsessions.

I believe the preoccupation with one's body is far more destructive than weight itself. Constantly spinning one's wheels on futile worry creates depression. This sullen existence prevents most people from enjoying life and living up to their potential as contributors to society. In addition, this lack of fulfillment reinforces the need to try and fill the emptiness with food—a useless cycle.

To help rid myself of this self-absorption, I worked on my self-esteem and body image. I recognized that all the trees in the forest are different in size and shape. Some have lots of leaves and branches while others have few. Some are tall and green and others shorter and wider and less colorful. Some are even tall and wide. Yet, all of the diversity in contour is what gives the forest its form. Acres of the same kind of evergreen trees in rows makes a Christmas tree farm, not a forest. On some level, I recognized that I belong to the majestic creation of the woods. I was proud to take my place with the mulberry bushes instead of regretting not having been born a cypress.

### *Make Peace with Who You Are... And Who You Are Not*

I'd always been unhappy about who I was because I believed I was supposed to reject myself. This message came to me loud and clear from the world around me. After all, I was fat.

Self-esteem includes body image, although body image is not the only factor for determining self-respect and pride. Poor self-esteem is:

- Motivated by the approval of others. In other words, a person with poor self-esteem measures herself by others' standards,
- Based on unrealistically high standards.

Psychology and self-help books tell you how important it is to have good self-esteem, but they fail to tell you how to develop it. By the time you are through with this book, you will learn how to stop using your body as a weapon to beat yourself up emotionally. If you're like most women who have suffered with weight and body-image issues, you've probably spent time feeling bad about it and attempting to diet and exercise the bad feelings away.

More than likely, you also had to deal with the humiliation of failure to change yourself. Once you recovered from the defeat, you gathered the courage to try again only to fail again. Stop and think about how this cycle has taken up an unbelievable amount of time away from living and enjoying life!

Now imagine, for just a few moments, that your body is perfectly acceptable. You totally trust that your body exists to support you in your life endeavors. Now you are free to use your time to enjoy yourself. You can pursue a hobby or perhaps devote yourself to a new career. What would you like to do? Because this change in self-acceptance will give you more time to foster interests, you have ample time to explore them now. Techniques to develop good self-esteem begin with "Body Image Focus Shift" in the Appendix. Good self-esteem is:

- Motivated by self-satisfaction.
- Reinforced by action.
- Based on realistic goals.
- Acceptance of small defeats as a need to work harder.

### *Whose Rules of Beauty Are These Anyway*

I remember a Twilight Zone episode that drove home the point that beauty rests in one's own perspective. The scene opened with a woman in a hospital bed, her face completely bandaged. Throughout most of the scene, the doctors and nurses talked about how much they hoped the surgery helped improve this poor woman's appearance. The feeling of pity prevailed, and the audience could only imagine how hideous she must have been. Finally, at the end of the episode, they unwrapped the bandages, and the hospital staff gasped in horror. The surgery did not work, as the woman's face remained the same. The camera moved in for a close-up of the woman. Her face glowed with stunning beauty that would be the envy of any woman in our society. The faces of the doctors and nurses had been hidden from the audience's view until this telling moment. Then the camera zoomed in to the hospital staff; we see unsightly features on utterly grotesque faces.

Self-esteem develops from what others think of us and what we learn to think of ourselves. We internalize things from society's attitudes and those of the significant people in our lives. The key word is learn because what has been learned can be re-evaluated.

The woman in the Twilight Zone episode viewed herself as ugly because others believed her to be. In much the same way, our society has shaped our attitudes toward body size and weight.

Has society always been so brutal to women? Were women always obsessed with fat? Is it a God-given curse that we've had to learn to live with it? Or is it created and perpetuated by society as merely pollution of the soul? Is it something we can clean up like the garbage in our rivers and the smoke in our air? I believe it is. First it's important to look at how and when it began.

> ***Destructive attitudes toward body size are created and perpetuated by society as merely a pollution of the soul.***

Art forms such as the clay figure called the Woman from Willendorf and the classic Venus de Milo showed women who undoubtedly weighed about two hundred pounds. Women were round and voluptuous and that was how it was supposed to be. When fertility was valued, large bellies and hips, an indication of fruitfulness, were beloved. The epitome of worship of large, rounded women occurred during the time of Rubens, who painted women as revered for their ample figures.

Prior to the 1860's, clothes were fitted to each individual body. A woman with larger hips had her dressmaker adjust the garment to accommodate her. She was not expected to change her shape to fit the dress. Industrialization, batch production, and mass marketing of dresses eroded the concept of catering to an individual customer's figure. In 1863, Ellen Butterick developed the dressmaker's pattern. Sometime after this, the wearer was then required to fit the pre-patterned garment not the other way around. Thus, the "ideal" figure was born.

Women's magazines continued to proliferate this fairy tale. In 1918, Vogue magazine printed a statement that linked fat as worse than criminal: "There is one crime against the modern ethics of beauty which is unpardonable; far better it is to commit any number of petty crimes than to be guilty of growing fat." Still today, fat as a crime is perpetuated in most women's magazines and the situation is getting worse. A generation ago, the average model weighed 8 percent less than the average woman. In 1999, models were 23 percent smaller.

The media bombard the public with pictures of extraordinarily good-looking women. This has an adverse effect on the average-looking person. In an experiment to determine the affect idealized models have on self-image, two groups viewed photos. The first group looked at pictures of better-than-average-looking people. The second group viewed photos of average-looking people. People in each group were then asked to evaluate their own looks. Not surprising, the group that had been exposed to the better-looking people judged themselves to be less attractive than the group that saw the average-looking people. Yet we encourage women's magazines to show us the "ideal image." They print it, and we beat ourselves over the head trying to achieve it.

American women seem to feel that excess weight is a moral issue, says Peter Stearns, professor of history at Carnegie Mellon University in Pittsburgh and author of Fat

History, a comparison of French and American eating habits. The French are not as likely to feel troubled about a few extra pounds. Some Parisian women said they felt "bien dans sa peau" -comfortable in their skin even if they need to lose a few kilos. They admit to feeling pretty even though they may be a few pounds overweight. One woman went on to admit that having a perfect body was not a sign of femininity in France.

### *Changing the Rules*

The theory of the hundredth monkey, based on scientific observation, suggests that if one monkey begins to do something differently, another monkey will follow suit. This theory began when a scientist observed a monkey wash a sweet potato in water. Another monkey saw the first one perform this new task and did the same thing. After a time, monkeys everywhere were doing this. In other words, if after a period of time, one hundred of these animals do something differently, others make the same change, even those that have no direct contact with the ones that started the new behavior. A significant change will occur in any species when the numbers are stacked.

Based on this theory, we only need a hundred of us to accept ourselves and our bodies, whatever our size. Therefore, we have the key to change the world. We will no longer feel brutalized by society's criticisms. Perhaps then we can get on with learning how to find happiness and fulfillment and letting our bodies find their right natural size.

### *The Happiness Commandment*

I'm struck by the wisdom of Richard Bach in his work, "Illusions: The Adventures of a Reluctant Messiah." The prophet is speaking to the multitude:

> *And he said unto them, "If a man told God that he wanted most of all to help the suffering world, no matter the price to himself, and God answered and told him what he must do, should he do as he is told?"*
>
> *"Of course Master!" cried the many. "It should be pleasure for him to suffer the tortures of hell itself, should God ask it!"*
>
> *"And what would you do," the Master said unto the multitude, "if God spoke directly to your face and said, 'I command that you be happy in the world, as long as you live.' What would you do then?"*
>
> *And the multitude was silent, not a voice, not a sound was heard upon the hillsides, across the valleys where they stood.*

Why is it that the simple concept that we deserve happiness escapes so many of us? The silence of the crowd indicates that they cannot believe that personal happiness can be God's wish for them. Yet they are eager to believe personal sacrifice is their duty, no matter the price.

The very definition of self-esteem includes the feeling of being worthy of happiness. Self-esteem can be defined as: "confidence in our ability to think and to cope with the basic challenges of life, as well as confidence in our right to be happy, the feeling of being worthy, deserving, and to enjoy the fruits of our efforts."

When we have good self-esteem, it allows us to be creative, productive, and joyful in becoming all that we are meant to be. Self-hatred is the enemy. Many persist in berating themselves about their lack of willpower to stay on a diet. It is as if they believe the thrashing will somehow transform this ugly, fat, person into a worthwhile, slim person; as if being slim is the criterion for making a person worthwhile. Not only does being slim not work, but it brings about even more discontent.

The few times I attempted to lose weight, I put more negative focus on my body than when I left myself alone to be myself. I'd spend time looking in the mirror at the places I needed to carve away more fat. The more weight I lost, the more I looked at my body and the more I found fault. Weight loss led to more obsession about my inadequacy, not less. And wasn't poor self-esteem the reason I wanted to lose weight in the first place? I ended up feeling worse about myself instead of better. To accept the doctrine that weight loss was essential, made me feel that I wasn't good enough as I was. This self-consciousness came from an expectation of perfection promoted by our society. Seeking acceptance from others by trying to satisfy a perfect image defeats the goal.

How do we broaden the scope of our identity? How do we include other aspects of ourselves on which to base our value and good feelings? How do we put physical appearance into perspective? If you're sick and tired of drowning in the negativity of thoughts about your body, try the exercises that start with "Food Meditation" in the Appendix. They are designed to help you discover your true values. To be happy, spend your time living your true values, not those you think you should live dictated by society.

## *Get A Life*

*Living Life Values: The grass may be greener on the other side, but you still have to mow it.*

Because I spent my childhood focused on food and my body, I robbed myself of time and energy to explore what was important in life. Now when I think of my youth, I remember the ice cream store across the street and the first time I bought a root beer for myself with my own money and the bakery that made black and white cookies. Unfortunately, these were the highlights—memories of food. Something was missing... a life.

Once I liberated myself from the obsession, I had to work to develop other interests. I didn't know what I valued. You may identify. If so, turn to "Life Values" in the Appendix to help you realize a world for yourself beyond dieting. Here's the story of how I discovered mine.

When I was in my pre-teens, I longed for more time with my mother. She was progressive for those times. Most women stayed at home and took care of the kids. She was a vibrant person and had a strong financial need to work outside the home. One day I suggested that it was more important to have her at home with me even if we had to live in an apartment instead of a house.

Although I now understand the reality of the need to work, I didn't understand then. I just saw it as an external thing that took away from my happiness.

We had had a beautiful back yard. Because of time demands on my parents, the landscaping was neglected. Flowers died and were left dried and brown in the ground. Trees and bushes became entwined and mangled. No one ever sat on the grass or enjoyed the fresh air. To me this was a waste. You work to buy the yard, but because you work, you have no time to enjoy it. I decided that I'd never get caught in that trap. And I haven't.

Because good self-esteem is motivated by self-satisfaction, and because a person who thinks well of herself will seek activities to fulfill this basic need, I had to seek to understand my true nature.

I've learned that I'm most happy when I have plenty of unstructured time and I'm not obsessing with my body. It is then that I am at my most creative, and I feel free to be myself. Because of the vow I took never to get caught up in externals (the yard/work cycle), I have lived a life of peace. My values were to have money for certain physical comforts (not to be confused with status). I wanted a house with a back yard to enjoy the peacefulness. I have that, and although it's smaller than I'd like, it satisfies my personal needs, not the idea of the type I should want. I even have a covered swing for relaxing and reading. I wanted a room where I could sit quietly and write. My desk sits beneath a window overlooking the wonderfully peaceful yard. I hear birds chirping even now in the early morning as I write these words. I live my dream life. That's not to say I don't want a bigger house with more room. If that becomes available to me, that's great. But I know what my values are. I know what makes me happy and content, and I spend my time, energy and money on just those things. My life enables me to spend time with my family and on my writing. Good self-esteem for me comes when I spend my time on those things I value most. Would that also be true for you?

Please understand that I am not making a value judgment about status. It just isn't worth the time for me. I am basically an introvert. I spend my time internally, therefore, having something to show externally serves little purpose. However, for some, prestige is valuable and worth the investment. They are involved with people who share this lifestyle, therefore, the prestige gives them a sense of belonging to that group. For these people, self-esteem is enhanced because it satisfies their true values and their needs.

The first three exercises in "Life Values" will help you to define your values and their relative priorities in your life.

### *Stop "Shoulding" on Yourself*

All of your "Should's" are usually based on unchallenged values. You assimilate life values unconsciously from things you hear and see as you grow up. You have accepted them without consciously looking at them and deciding if they are right for you.

Start with a premise of no shoulds, only wants and choices. Nothing is intrinsically good or bad about anything. It is all a matter of the value we choose to put on it.

If you continuously find yourself not wanting to spend your time cleaning your house, for example, perhaps you value your time for other things.

The "Life Values" exercises will help you re-evaluate your own. After completing the exercise and thinking about your values, you're beginning to develop a life beyond your body and food, and it's safe to go on to the Body Image chapter. You will more likely keep it in better perspective.

*To enhance self-esteem, order a self-hypnosis tape. See the listings in the Appendix of this book, on pages 199 ff.*

## Chapter 2—Body Image:

# You Are Not Your Body

*The best and most beautiful things in the world cannot be seen or even touched. They must be felt with the heart.*

Helen Keller

Jamie came to me with poor body image. I asked her to think of someone who liked her body the way it was. She said her boyfriend did. I asked her to find the difference between her perspective and her boyfriend's. She always looked at her body by focusing in on one detail at a time and criticizing it. For example, she'd look at her thighs and decide they were too fat or decide her breasts were too small. On the other hand, her boyfriend looked at her body as a whole picture and from a slightly further vantage point. He saw her total being as attractive. I asked her to close her eyes and imagine looking at herself on a TV screen from six feet away. From this view, she liked what she saw.

I approach my body in much the same way as my life values. Sure it would be nice to be slim. Like spending money for a big-screen TV that I had no time or energy to enjoy, the pursuit of that body would make me obsessive.

Obsession is another word for self-absorbed, and self-involvement definitely distracts from my happiness.

## *Put Body Size in Perspective*

### *Well-Rounded Happiness*

I have read several of Geneen Roth's books (see the Resources section for these and other recommended readings). She has a belief similar to mine. If you eat with awareness of your body's needs, you can be thin. She has, in fact, attained slimness and maintained it for years. She has eaten chocolate and still enjoys a trim body.

Although this has not been the result for me, I can live with myself anyway. I encounter a conflict only when I come up against society. When I think of venturing out in the world to promote my philosophy and my book, I cringe a little. I will probably be criticized by some as not having slimmed down enough to be any authority on the subject. I do know, however, once I get past the initial impression, I will be met with women who desperately want to know how to stop obsessing and find their own paths to happiness. For some, a slender body will be part of it. Yet, their body size will no longer be the only source for happiness. Others will find their body changing only slightly. But just as with those whose slim bodies only proportionately contribute to their well-being, larger-sized women will find a well-rounded source for happiness (pun intended!).

### *Ugly Duckling or Developing Swan*

Most people approach exercise and dieting as if something is wrong with their bodies. They are striving for perfection. To be perfect is not to be flawless. To be perfect is to be developed, ripened, or matured. Our bodies are not damaged goods; but rather green, hard, and under-ripened fruit. To try to become flawless is to reinforce a negative self-image. You can't change "what is." If, in fact you are an ugly duckling, then you are and there's nothing you can do about it. Instead, view yourself in terms of an underdeveloped swan. Your body is not damaged, but rather developing.

Are you one who is hoping for perfection when the diet is over? Are you putting your life on hold until you are finished? When you get to a magical number on a bathroom scale, will you stop everything. and get off the merry-go-round? Has all that you've worked for then vanished? Try changing your mind-set. Think of having the body you want as an on-going process, not a destination. Enjoy the ride. Imagine a trip through the mountains. Doesn't part of the pleasure come from the relaxation of the drive and looking at the scenery?

Ask yourself how you can enjoy your body just as it is. You'll find this easier to do if you make a focus shift. Instead of looking for appearance as the reward, concentrate on how you feel. Do the things that make your body feel good today. For myself, a brief stroll around the block will automatically increase my mental and physical relaxation. This works as an immediate reward. (Notice I said a "brief stroll," not vigorous exercise.)

Most people place undue demands on themselves. Exercise has its time and place, which will be addressed in the chapter on the Joy of Exercise. To make yourself feel good, make sure you choose something that you enjoy doing rather than considering it just another thing on your list of things that you have to do.

- •Think of having the body you want as a process, not a destination.
- •Instead of the focus on how your body looks as the reward, concentrate on how you can make your body feel good.
- •Ask yourself how you can enjoy your body as it is just for today.

## *The Salieri Complex:*

### *Jealousy Will Drive You Nuts*

Antonio Salieri, a composer, obsessed about Mozart's magnificent musical talent. "If only I could make music that way, life would be grand," he thought. This haunting jealousy drove him to absolute misery. Some speculate that his extreme discontent drove him to a mental institution.

This same compelling urge often fuels a woman's self-hatred syndrome. She judges herself according to standards of others. Her envy forces her to misdirect her efforts and energy to a futile ride on the diet treadmill. Even the most intelligent of us can make ourselves feel stupid if we compare ourselves to Einstein. Yet most women continue to compare their looks to the doctored photos in fashion magazines.

Jealousy is pain caused by the thought of losing the loved object. In this case the loss is the loss of self-esteem. It is compounded by self-criticism in which the person blames herself for the loss. It is not completely based on reality, as it is disproportionate to the real circumstances.

My mother was quite overweight (although not as much as she perceived herself to be). When I was in my teens, she pointed out a trim attractive woman and joked, "Don't you just hate her?" The implication, of course, was that slim was so much better to be. She'd laugh to try and lighten the emotional load of feeling jealous and inferior. This was an assault to her self-esteem. I believe she tried to use this negativity to motivate herself (and perhaps me) to change. I felt indignant at the comparison.

This anger was my saving grace. Had I been prone to agree, it would most likely have sent me spiraling into the insanity of futile dieting followed by defeat and despair. Thank God, I have an "oppositional" personality (the need to do the opposite of what my mother wanted me to do). Either that or some innate wisdom taught me that nothing was wrong with me as I was. I didn't have to compete to be skinny just because someone else felt she should.

Personally, I don't get it. I don't see the attraction to thinness. Sure, I wouldn't mind being a size smaller than I am. But it's no big deal that I'm not. In fact, I find women with some roundness more visually appealing anyway.

And yet, the emotional pain of feeling totally unaccepted by my mother deeply saddened me. I know now that this was not the intended message. My mother rejected herself and accepted an unrealistic and false image and projected this on to me. Yet it was difficult not to feel rejected.

How can we empower ourselves (and our daughters) to appreciate our own bodies even when they differ from the ideal? It is amazing... making peace with yourself can be quite slimming!

## *Body Image*

Self-esteem and body image develop, in part, from feedback from people around us. Unfortunately, my mother and aunt received negative feedback about themselves. They in turn passed it along to me. These personal influences and the unrealistic images portrayed by the media, set me up for defeat. Fortunately, I rebelled against being told that my body was not good enough because it didn't meet size expectations.

When I was about 20 years old, a simple experience helped me rise above my negative body image. I had a close friend who'd never had a weight problem. I talked to her about how I ought to lose weight. I felt rejected by men because of my size. One day she looked at me curiously. She said men would like to be with me because I was round and soft. She thought this would be attractive because my softness was comforting. She compared that to her body; her hipbones stuck out. She was sure they were uncomfortable because they poked at men when they cuddled.

What an awakening! This was the first time I'd ever heard anyone view my "fat" in a positive light. It was an

> ***She said she thought men would like me because I was round and soft. What an awakening! This was the first time I ever heard anyone view my "fat" in a positive light.***

opportunity I'd been waiting for. I took the ball and ran with it. I continued from that moment to reframe all the past ideas about my body. I was determined to find positive points of view. Not surprising, from that moment on, I found men who were attracted to me as I was. Once I had a positive perspective, I projected it. Others felt it and were drawn to the attitude I conveyed. This demeanor made me attractive. I was finally able to relax with myself and enjoy acceptance from men. A simple shift in my own disposition, and suddenly I attracted a different type of person. Try the "Body Image Focus Shift" exercise in the Appendix.

### *Boost Your Body Image*

Often, we are fatter between our ears than in our physical bodies. We hold images of our appearance in our mind's eye, images that are often distorted. These erroneous pictures and ideas drive us to the irrational pursuits of the idealized body. We often exaggerate the importance of particular parts of our bodies. Such "selective attention" also makes us blind to our attractive features. This chapter will show how to adjust your body image like fine tuning the color on your television.

Success breeds success. Yet we approach body image as if something is wrong with it rather than enhancing the good that exists. The following story brings this point home.

A second incident occurred about having been told I was short-waisted which challenged my ability to keep my self-esteem intact. I was having a dress custom made. The dressmaker struggled to find how to fit the waist part of the dress to the appropriate place in my middle. She made remarks about how strangely high my waist was. Enough to make anyone self-conscious!

Fortunately, my positive thinking pulled me through. I looked down and reminded myself about my relatively long legs for someone only 5'5." My legs are as long as those of some people who are 5'8." Now I had always been told that long legs were quite attractive. I knew that I had a choice. I could focus my attention on my high waist, or I could concentrate on the positive feature. Once I began to take pride in my lower length, I stood taller and I projected body confidence.

Nothing is intrinsically good or bad about anything. We choose the value we place on something. When we start with a neutral premise, it is easier to lift ourselves into a positive thought process then when starting out negatively. The exercise on page 155 will help you to nurture positive thought processes about your body.

### *Treat Yourself: A Positive Mental Body Image*

One day my bra felt slightly snug. I decided to clip it on the next hook. I then went about my day and forgot I'd loosened it. Because it felt loose, throughout the day I found myself noticing that I felt much slimmer, which made me feel good. I also noticed that I ate less. I felt as if I were making food choices based on a self-image of a slimmer body. I wasn't concerned about trying to control my food choices. It just seemed like a natural thing to do. When I felt good and viewed myself in a positive light, I treated myself well.

I don't know if my ability to shun public opinion and society's view about fat and weight was because I was rebellious. Perhaps it was because a part of me is an introvert. Or maybe I became an introvert out of a need to shun others' negativity. But I do know that I enjoy my own company and this enables me to feel good about myself at any size regardless of society's view. (Only, of course, if I am taking reasonably good care to eat well and exercise moderately and keep myself in decent shape).

I developed a way to go within myself to find comfort and acceptance. Before I developed this ability to seek solace from within, I had to rebel. My mother attempted to project her poor body image onto me. My resistance to this was my saving grace. Her poor body image influence came across loud and clear with her constant reminders of how an item of clothing needed improvement. This became an issue of contention between us. What ever I wore, she seemed to be focused on the negativity of my body. (Her poor attempt, albeit motivated by good intentions of wanting me to improve my appearance so I'd be more accepted by others, prompted me to reject her ideas).

She focused on how my body looked. I focused on how my body felt. Bicycle riding always made me feel free and strong. Roller skating stirred my imagination into feeling like I was flying. My childhood consisted of seeking every opportunity for these joyous experiences of my body. When I lived within the experience of my body, I enjoyed it and felt good about it. It was only when I looked in the mirror or someone brought attention to my appearance that I became unhappy with my body.

We all internalize negative experiences like these and allow them to influence our opinions of ourselves unconsciously. Imagine if I'd accepted my mother's viewpoint of my body. (Fortunately, I didn't.) However, there are many other negative experiences from my childhood that float around in my mind unchallenged.

It is only when I bring these to the surface that I can confront them and decide which ones to throw out and which ones to keep. See page 160 for the exercise to exorcise these ghosts of the past.

## *Role Models*

It is no secret that public personalities help create a culture obsessed with thin. When television and movies portray women with perfect bodies, it is no wonder the rest of us feel we fall short of the mark. We set ourselves up for grave disappointment about our bodies and then wonder why we feel so negative. Until recently, the only role models we had were fashion models and public personalities that fit an idealized image. Finally, things are changing.

When I was a teen, I loved to dance. I had fantasies of becoming a dancer. But at a size 18, it didn't seem likely. Then I heard about Isadora Duncan. She was a large woman with a reputation for quite an original dance style. Bingo! I had a role model and was satisfied. However, had I not been able to accept the reality of my life and my body, I might have let myself become bitter and miserable.

I'd probably have cast off Isadora as not a valid role model or not even acknowledged her at all. I'd have continued my search for something that doesn't exist and experienced only empty yearning. This is how I see most American women: having a perpetual longing that plagues their souls. And why? Because they refuse to grow up and face life on life's terms. They want to continue to live in a fantasy world and look to false images as their heroines.

Funny! One of the most successful public personalities in America suffers from this "wannabe complex." Oprah Winfrey, with her dazzle, fame, and extraordinary accomplishments seems to fault herself for her body-type. There's probably not an American woman that doesn't hold her in such high esteem. To us she is a Beauty queen. And yet, to herself, she is not enough because her body does not meet the thin fairy princess image. Look at the awe in her eyes as she watches Dr. Phil McGraw tell how he too, has the secret to being slim. Just what we need, another guru to hold thinness up as a God to worship! In reference to thin people and in typical mock hate he laughs, "Don't you just hate them?" No, Phil, I don't. I don't even understand it.

*Just what we need... another guru to hold thinness up as a God to worship.*

That's like hating Mozart for his talent. It's not even remotely who I am. How could I have the audacity to compare myself to such brilliance? It's only when I think I have some chance of being like the person that I admire that I compare myself. This is a healthy sense of competition. It is healthy because it motivates me to reach it. Now if you ask me if I envy my piano-playing friends, the answer is "Yes, I do." I know that I have some talent and if I were to work at it, I could attain some level of keyboard expertise. This is a healthy challenge (See more on success through appropriate challenges in the section on keeping yourself motivated.) To try to be what you are not only serves to frustrate and intensify insecurity.

Insecure people choose unreasonably high standards, which lead to failure. Failure reinforces insecurity, which in turn leads to even more overcompensation by choosing unreasonably high standards. And the cycle continues. Does this frustration sound familiar? The antidote is to face your insecurity, choose reasonable challenges, and meet them. You will begin to feel better about yourself. After you have some success under your belt, you can build on it. To envy the flat body type when your body type tends to be round reinforces insecurity. Instead, find someone to respect and admire whose body type is similar to your own.

Let's talk about some role models who present a more practical image to admire. Women tend to put fashion models on a pedestal and try to emulate them.

Even Hollywood is coming around to accept beauty in its various sizes. Casting director Amy Jo Berman respects actresses who say, "To heck with it—this is how we look." Other signs point out that this industry is coming to accept rounder bodies. Hollywood producer David Foster says, "I'm aware of actresses looking more natural today than they did two, three, even four years ago." He worked

*"I'm never going to be thin and waif-like. The added pounds round you out. I love my body now that it's softer," says Sandra Bullock..*

with Catherine Zeta-Jones on 1998's Mask of Zorro, adding that this beauty "is not the skinny rail" kind of woman.

"I'm never going to be thin and waif-like," says actress Sandra Bullock. She says the added pounds "round you out. I love my body now that it's softer."

"I want to eat fun meals and laugh and enjoy myself," says actress Drew Barrymore. She even went so far as to show the sexy star of the movie Charlie's Angels heartily eating hamburgers and fries.

Celebrity fitness guru High Voltage supports Drew's attitude. She says of the actress, "She looks comfortable in her own skin."

Emme, one of the world's leading plus-size models, sets forth positive attitudes and practical tips. In her book, True Beauty, she makes some interesting points about size and acceptance. She tells of Marilyn Monroe's size sixteen figure at the height of her career, complete with rounded hips and a fleshy bottom. How can we use this effervescent public personality to encourage self-esteem and acceptance of all body types and sizes?

In her book, "Making it Big," fashion expert Jean Ducoffe shows how to look terrific at any size. She offers beauty, fashion, and grooming advice to help women become more alive, stunning, sexy, and secure. She proves you can be sensual, feminine and desirable at whatever size you are.

In my private hypnotherapy practice, people often come to me to lose weight. One invaluable lesson I try to instill is the need to find a reasonable role model.

"I don't know what size I should be, but I sure as heck know it's not the size I am," said Rachael.

"How do you know?" I asked.

"Well uh, it can't be okay to be this size," she stammered.

"Why not?" I asked.

"Well, because....I don't know."

I asked, "Is it possible you've been sold a bill of goods?"

"No, I don't think so. I just know it can't be okay to be the way I am," she continued.

"So you're sure something's wrong with the way you are?" I asked.

Thoughtfully she replied, "Well, hmmm! Now that you mention it, there is that lady wrestler named Chyna. She's pretty big but quite muscular. I know she's in great shape. You can just see the way she moves." After a moment of silent contemplation, Rachael said, "I guess I can be healthy and large."

For the first time, someone challenged her assumption about her size. She had spent her life feeling bad about herself when she actually was closer to what she ought to be than she thought. As a large-framed women of about 5'9", even when she was slimmer, Rachael weighed 150 pounds. It was unrealistic for her to expect to weigh much less than that. A lifetime of trying to squeeze herself into a smaller body ended that day, and her entire relationship to food changed. When she stopped emotionally beating herself for being what she was, her need for excessive food dwindled.

Have you heard the expression, "I'd never join a club that would have me as a member?" Has this been your attitude? Have you refused to admire someone just because she was larger than the ideal? Viable role models come in a variety of sizes. Find someone to hold in esteem. Of all the suggestions in this book, if you do only this one, you will be well ahead of the game.

## Chapter 3—Diet Myths:

# The Fat of the Matter and Other Diet Myths

Caryn had spent most of the previous ten years on a diet. As a result, she was two sizes larger than when she first began. Each period of restriction was followed by a binge. Her self-esteem was lower than ever. She hated herself for not having self-control. She viewed her inability to take charge of herself as flaw in her character. She constantly berated herself for not being able to stick to an eating plan.

It turned out, most of the time Caryn was starving herself. She had chosen a well thought-out and balanced diet, yet she spent many nights going to sleep feeling hungry. About an hour after breakfast she felt hungry again. It seemed that hunger was a constant companion. "It couldn't be anything wrong with the diet," she thought. "Weight Watchers is nationally recognized and accepted by most nutritionists as a sound plan. Something must be wrong with me."

The only thing wrong with her was that she didn't listen to her body's signals. Caryn needed more food and her body told her so. I helped her integrate foods with more bulk. She ate more whole grains and beans. She finally felt that her body was getting enough nutrition. She felt satisfied. Her calorie intake was two to three times what it had been, yet she lost inches everywhere. Within several months she was wearing a smaller size. Once she learned the "Success for the Diet Dropout" method, she was careful not to restrict any type of food. Food deprivation triggers desire for excessive amounts of food. Sometimes deprivation plays havoc with our body chemicals and creates an authentic nutritional need. Thus, a person's attempt to gorge is a normal reaction to compensate for the lack.

Food restriction plays havoc with the natural cycle of nerve chemicals, says Sarah Leibowitz Ph.D., professor of neurobiology at Rockefeller University in New York City. Research with laboratory rats supports this claim. These animals were forced to eat a restrictive diet. Once the restriction was removed, their appetites were insatiable. They gorged and increased their consumption of fat from a typical 35 percent of calories to as much as 60 percent of calories.

In addition to that experiment, another done on healthy average height and weight volunteers during World War II proved how semi-starvation created an intolerable miserable disposition and an overriding sense of hunger that could not be appeased. These men started out eating 3,500 calories daily. After three months, they were rationed 1,750 calories daily.

Men who'd been quite cheerful became irritable, lethargic, apathetic, argumentative, and food-obsessed. Two men had emotional breakdowns. The experiment ended sooner than planned for fear of emotional crisis; had the men been required to sustain the reduced calorie diet. Afterward, the volunteers' daily intake went up to 4,000 calories, 500 more than they started with.

***Men who'd been quite cheerful became irritable, lethargic, and food-obsessed when their daily calorie intake went from 3,500 to 1,750 calories per day.***

Their insatiable appetite was apparent even four months after they had freedom to eat as they wished. In Dr. William Bennett's book, "The Dieters Dilemma," he writes, "Thus, even though their bodies were taking in considerable food energy, the profound psychological alteration that semi-starvation had produced remained with them."

Still other times the loss results in an emotional reaction, says Judith Wurtman, Ph.D., head of the Nutrition and Behavior Studies Group at the Clinical Research Center and research scientist in the department of Brain and Cognitive Science at MIT. She concludes that we experience "two types of hunger: physical which is driven by our body's need for nourishment, and psychological hunger, which is propelled by our need for comfort and solace."

Research shows that physiological responses drive both these needs. Both the physical hunger and the emotional hunger have their basis in nature. In her research, Wurtman observed, "stress and its associated moods provoked a hunger for sweet or starchy carbohydrates." The body knows what the brain needs and will do what ever is necessary to supply it—even if it means eating certain foods after a vow to abstain.

Yet some people persist in opposing the natural order of things by dieting. When they cannot maintain this level of deprivation, they feel shamed. It is as though they have done something immoral. It feels bad when the drive to eat overrides the desire to sustain a diet. With the failure, depression often results, further fueling the need to eat.

Jonathan came to me, upset with himself that he couldn't go 24 hours without eating. He used this unrealistic expectation to berate himself. He viewed himself as weak-willed and hated himself for this. I wonder if he would have been as critical if he couldn't hold his breath for 15 minutes. This example of working against one's own natural instincts is quite obvious. However, those who want to go on a diet don't realize that the restriction of a forced eating plan taps into the same mechanism: opposition to nature.

> *Jonathon hated himself because he couldn't go 24 hours without eating. I wonder if he would have been as critical if he couldn't hold his breath for 15 minutes?*

I knew of a man who enjoyed a reputation of being able to help people lose weight. Because of his success, people who had tried to gain weight and failed asked for his guidance. He agreed to help them beef up their bodies if they would follow his advice to the letter. The weight consultant gave each of the underweight participants a 1000-calorie diet. He instructed them to stick to this eating plan for four weeks. Their mouths fell open in surprise. "We can't gain weight eating three times the amount of calories. How do you expect us to increase our size on this?"

After a bit of persuasion, he convinced them to trust him and try it. After four weeks, they were consumed by thoughts of food. They began to eat, as they never did before. Their appetites were insatiable. (Does this sound familiar?) Within a short time, the increased body size they wanted was theirs without any problem.

***Stomach Owners' Instruction Manual:***
*When Hungry, Eat; When Not Hungry, Don't Eat*

Janie was in the process of re-learning how to read her body's need for food. She had difficulty with eating at night. In the first week, she noticed a change in her night binge eating. She had a spoonful of ice cream instead of the typical bowl. But she still had difficulty allowing herself to eat when she was hungry. She was upset with herself for eating a half of a turkey sandwich one evening about 7:00 p.m. The conversation went like this:

*Dr. G.Were you hungry?*

*J. Yes, but I still could have tried to not eat.*

*Dr. G. What would have been the point of that?*

*J. Then I would have been exercising some sense of control.*

*Dr. G.It is one thing to control the compulsion to eat when you are not hungry. It is quite an other to try and control hunger.*

I then proceeded to tell her the story about the young man who wanted to abstain from eating for 24 hours. She could see the absurdity in this need. She said his expectations were unrealistic. Yet she couldn't quite see that her own demand was just as impractical.

If your body is hungry, eat. If it's not hungry, don't eat. The urge to eat is a force as strong as the current of the river. Accept this fact, and you will stop resisting this natural need and find an alternative to dieting. Exactly what are these natural instincts?

### *Search for Serotonin Sends Signals to Snack*

Serotonin is a brain chemical associated with a level of calm. Low serotonin levels create irritability. When nutrients from foods are digested in suitable amounts, this chemical is produced. When serotonin is active in the brain in appropriate quantities, the brain signals the body that its need for food is satisfied. Sometimes, the serotonin level is inappropriately low. When this happens, the impulse to supply extra nutrients motivates the individual to eat more.

Stress is one cause of low serotonin in the brain. An experiment at the University of Michigan studied stress in women and the need to eat. Participants gathered in a room and watched two different movies. Researchers provided an ample supply of carbohydrate snacks (good sources of serotonin)—pretzels, candy, cookies etc. When they watched a stress-producing, gory, and gruesome film about accidents, the women ate twice as much as when they watched a bland movie about travel.

Michael Norden, M.D., is a noted psychiatrist and author of the book Beyond Prozac. He states that pre-clinical studies show that physical and psychological stresses immediately signal serotonin neurons to heighten serotonin release. If the stress lasts too long, it leads to serotonin depletion. Thus, stress drives the need for the nutrients that create serotonin activity. The individual then reaches for more food... and the cycle goes on.

Research shows a connection between low serotonin levels and aggression and impulsive behavior. In a study on Rhesus monkeys, monkeys with higher serotonin activity moved from branch to branch to shorten leaping distances. Those with low serotonin levels impulsively leaped far distances at heights where falls could prove fatal. This demonstrated an aggressive behavior toward oneself. People who berate themselves for being fat may be victims of this same aggressive mechanism.

We also know now that the process of eating is the brain's way of replenishing serotonin. This is done in two ways. The nutrients from food replenish the chemicals, and physical activity stimulates serotonin.

### *Calm Yourself with Repetitive Motion*

Research shows that repetitive motion such as chewing helps bring about higher serotonin activity. Dr. Barry Jacobs from Princeton University has discovered that some types of muscle movement generate more serotonin than others. Repetitive motions are most effective, particularly chewing or licking. Not surprising then, eating is a viable choice for helping a person relax.

Your body knows it needs serotonin and knows that licking or chewing will stimulate its release. With this knowledge, doesn't it make sense that your instinct is to reach for food? It's as reasonable as gasping for air when you're short of breath. Is this perhaps a form of self-medication? If so, doesn't this make a further case for self-acceptance and learning to work with what we have instead of fighting it? Not that I advocate eating as a means for a release of stress. I am suggesting that the instinct to do so is a physiological response. Therefore, I suggest some understanding and compassion. With the knowledge that repetitive movements help serotonin levels, we can then re-direct our impulse to eat when we are not hungry—toward other types of activity such as walking, knitting, or any other repetitive motion activity. (More discussion on this in exercise and stress-relief chapters.)

I am aware even as I write this that I have a thought that I need food. I check in with my stomach and notice I am not hungry. Suddenly I realize that this is a signal that I am stressed. This simple awareness allows me to take charge of my stress and redirect it. I am now conscious that the writing I have been doing for the last hour has gotten me keyed up. A break from the computer is what I need, not food. Allowing myself to take the impulse to eat as a sign that something else is going on helps me to utilize the knowledge. Because I applied understanding to myself instead of self-blame, I was able to use the technique of awareness. If I'd hated myself for the food thought, I would have cut myself off from my physical and emotional experience. More than likely, I would have reached for food instead of solving the real problem.

Stress is partly responsible for the depletion of serotonin. Dieting itself causes stress. "Dieting is one of the most physiologically and psychologically stressful things a person can do," says Pamela Peeke, M.D., assistant clinical professor of medicine at University of Maryland School of Medicine. "It reduces metabolism and energy levels, leads to mood swings and impaired immunity." The guilt we feel when we eat things we believe we shouldn't also cause stress. This stress causes overeating; what then, is the answer? Reducing stress in general is the obvious answer. The not-so-obvious answer is reducing the stress associated with dieting and with the guilt of not dieting.

Sometimes the best route to get from point A to point B is not the shortest or most direct. Dieting might seem to be the most direct path to weight loss. On the surface, it makes sense: go from point A to point B. But here's a metaphor that shows a different strategy.

> *Sometimes the best route to get from point A to point B is not the shortest or most direct. But, in the long run, if you want to lose weight, maintain your focus on reducing your stress. Don't increase stress by dieting. It will only add to the delays in reaching your destination. When the anxiety is gone, you will feel more powerful over food choices.*

Imagine you are in an airplane in a San Diego airport and want to fly to Hawaii. The logical direction to take is west. However, by going west immediately, you would end up crashing into the plane beside you. In order to get out of the airport, first you must go south. Then you can head west to your ultimate destination. In much the same way, if you want to lose weight, maintain your focus on reducing your stress. Don't increase it by dieting. You will arrive at your destination more safely and easily. When the anxiety is gone, you will feel more powerful over food choices.

### *Can Dieting Cause Stress?*

An experiment in Finland proved that dieting can cause stress. Twelve hundred business executives were at high risk for cardiac disease from obesity, hypertension, high cholesterol levels, or heavy smoking. They were asked to follow a strict regimen of a low-fat diet, medical exams, and access to information about potential risks. Another group of individuals with similar high-risk factors was left to do what ever they liked. After five years, death rates were higher for the strictly monitored group. Dr. Deepak Chopra speculates, "The only explanation seems to be that the stress and worry created by following an unfamiliar 'healthy' lifestyle more than canceled any benefits of the lifestyle itself."

I remember when I first decided to let go of dieting as an option. It was amazing to notice how much less hungry I was. Because I felt less stressed, my body was not depleting serotonin, and I lost my need to replenish this chemical through food.

- Repetitive motion such as chewing helps bring about higher levels of soothing brain chemical activity.
- Accept the need to eat as an instinctive and natural attempt to self-comfort. It is as involuntary and normal as breathing, so don't berate yourself.

- Accept the impulse to eat when not hungry as a sign that an unmet need is demanding your attention. Find out what that need is. (See exercise on fulfilling unmet needs, page 169.)
- Gradually integrate different types of repetitive motion activities into your life such as walking, knitting, swimming, etc.

### *Lose the Lazy Language*

Modern scientists developed a theory to answer the weight problem mystery, the "set-point theory," which gained national attention. The body has a survival mechanism and will not starve itself to death. As a result, when one decreases food intake, the body's defense mechanism slows down its metabolism in order to make efficient use of the food it is being given. Thus, it requires less food to maintain itself. This has become accepted as a law of nature, yet here we are, still beating our heads against the wall trying to trick the integrity of physics. To me, it is like saying we can learn to walk on water.

When I was about 12 or 13, a family friend told me that she had compassion for thin people who tried to gain weight. Their metabolism tended to work off the extra food so that the body would maintain itself. She went on to explain that this inclination to maintain the status quo was unfortunate, but it had its basis in nature and the individual didn't have control over this. She then proceeded to berate herself for not being able to reduce the size of her body. She would say, "Why can't I just control myself and stop stuffing my face?" Hmmmm! Had it not occurred to her that the same law of nature applied to her? The erroneous attitude that fat people choose to be this way, that we are fat because we eat too much, that we are lazy and lack the character needed to resist temptation is pervasive in our culture. It is damaging to the self-esteem and perpetuates prejudice.

To think of the reward, a slim body, works in much the same way. Such thoughts drain you of the power to focus on the good behavior. Many have succeeded for periods of time. They reach their weight goal, but because the reward (staying slim) becomes the focus, they lose track of the real goal: to maintain good food and exercise behavior in order to maintain good health so they can enjoy life.

The main purpose of your body is to allow you a vehicle with which to experience life. This is the real reward of physical fitness. When my body is well taken care of, I find my senses are more alive and awake. To experience the joy in life becomes harder when my body isn't well. When my motivation to eat well and exercise comes from this philosophy, I succeed readily. When I pursue a false goal, to feed only the ego with good looks, I fail. Like phony stones made to look like diamonds, I crush under the pressure to maintain the facade.

*The main purpose of my body is to allow me a vehicle with which to experience life. When I pursue a false goal, to feed only the ego with good looks, I fail. Like phony stones made to look like diamonds, I crush under the pressure to maintain the facade.*

## Chapter 4—Food:

# Food Is Not Your Enemy or Your Friend

*He said, "...Come to the edge."*
*They said, "...We are afraid."*
*He said, "...Come to the edge."*
*They came.*
*He pushed them.*
*They flew.*

Author unknown

One morning I decided I wanted to go out for a big breakfast of eggs and toast and hash brown potatoes. I immediately heard my stomach shout out, "Nooooo!" My stomach wanted to stay home and relax and have a warm soothing bowl of cream of wheat. My mouth wanted the taste of the big breakfast but my stomach wasn't up for it. I stopped and closed my eyes to get in touch with what was going on.

My mind wanted to escape the tension I was feeling. With a knee-jerk reaction, I sought the distraction of being in a restaurant with people and activity all around me. Yet a part of me wanted to deal with the stress with a healthy escape. Relaxation was my true need and I decided to honor it that morning. I made myself some cream of wheat and went out in my peaceful backyard to listen to the birds as I read a book and sat in my swing. The rest of my day went far better than had I decided to ignore my stress or eaten the breakfast I neither really wanted or needed.

Food is food. It is not your friend or your enemy. You might want to reconsider its place in your life. Does dieting become a feeling of punishment because you are deprived? Does going off the diet become—at first—a reward because you eat the foods you love; then eventually more punishment because you hate what it's doing to you and your body?

The true purpose of food is to give you fuel to energize your body. In order to stimulate interest in taking in food, nature has provided us with taste buds. Therefore, to enjoy food is part of the process. Food is not any more of a reward than a bright sunny day or any more of a punishment than a rainy cold day. The weather is there to enjoy when you can. If you need to work in an office on a sunny day, does it mean you are being punished because you can't go out and enjoy it? Of course not; it is just part of life. So too is food. When you are hungry, go ahead and enjoy food. When you are not, food is irrelevant. This chapter will show you how to reconnect with the pleasure of food without misusing it.

### ***The Control Paradox:***
*Let Go and You'll Be in Control*

Elliott Blass, Ph.D., at Cornell University, speculates that appetite-regulating brain chemicals go berserk when people attempt restrictive diets or reduce their fat or sugar intake too quickly. Thus, food restriction leads to a binge. The antidote, then, is to change eating patterns gradually.

The first step to change your eating patterns is awareness. Many people tend to go unconscious when they eat. They become preoccupied. Thinking, reading, talking, watching TV, or some other activity distracts them from what they are doing. They cut themselves off from the experience of their body. Consequently, they shove much more food into their mouths than they would if they had been aware. The sense of satisfaction goes unnoticed. For many people, even feeling full does not stop the eating. It only stops with the physical pain of an overly full stomach or the emotional pain of realizing how much food has been consumed. By then, people feel guilty, and it is too late to change things. A technique called "food meditation" will teach you a new type of awareness: One that will make a shift in your internal experience. It will offer you a way to take charge of yourself and get in touch with your experience of food, your body, and satisfaction. In addition, it will help you develop some internal controls.

Imagine Jell-O represents something very important to you. Picture your favorite color Jell-O in the palm of your hand. Because it is important to you, you want to hold onto it so you tighten your fingers around it. What happens? The Jell-O squishes through your fingers. You lose the very thing you want to hold.

Now imagine that same valuable Jell-O. This time, you gently curl your fingers, forming a cradle. Now what happens? Because you didn't try too hard for control, you had control and were able to hold onto that valuable item. The same is true with control of your diet or body size. Let go!

These internal controls, once you develop them, will work far better and for longer periods than the dictates of a diet. When the external controls of the diet are removed, all control is lost. Diets are like girdles. Once you wear them, your body loses its muscle tone. Your body becomes so accustomed to the external control that the stomach muscles relax and lose their strength. Exercise is required in order to strengthen them again. In much the same way, food meditation is one exercise that will fortify your internal muscle control.

> *Diets are like girdles. Once you wear one, your stomach loses its muscle tone. Food meditation is one exercise that will strengthen your internal controls over food. You will learn to enjoy food more and discover you are satisfied with less.*

Food meditation is a process that begins by allowing yourself the time and the opportunity to find your level of satisfaction. It allows for a slow steady change that gives your body time to adjust without going haywire. You will learn to enjoy food more and discover that you are satisfied with less. The more you give yourself the freedom to take pleasure in eating without the guilt, the more you will be capable of finding your level of contentment.

When life revolves around trying to lose weight, guilt builds up. This guilt makes you want to deny your eating experience. It is no wonder you go unconscious when you eat-it feels like a shameful thing to do. It is crucial to let down your defenses when you do this technique. Otherwise, your self-consciousness and guilt will prevent you from the full experience. If you cut yourself off from your experience of eating, the moment of satisfaction will go unnoticed. In order to help you feel the freedom of this exercise, plan to do it at a time when you are alone, and you are free to be yourself.

The first time I had any inkling of what it felt like to be truly satisfied with the food I'd eaten was when I determined to let down my guard and eat freely. I'd been criticized about eating all my life. Because of this, letting go of my guilt was not easy. I instinctively knew that the emotional eating I'd been doing fed the need to eat more. I decided to try an experiment.

I was in high school at the time and chose a private place in a rarely used area of the cafeteria. I bought the foods I really wanted as opposed to those I thought I should eat. I'd had so much brainwashing about what foods a fat girl should and shouldn't eat, it was a miracle that I even knew what I wanted. I took the tray of food which included chocolate cake and spaghetti and sneaked behind a divider wall to eat and enjoy my food without the pressure of taunting comments from classmates. No one was watching me so I ate slowly and without pressure. I ate as much as I wanted and was sure to enjoy each bite. An interesting thing happened. I was satisfied at the end of the meal and not longing for more. This was something

I knew could happen (that's why I created this exercise to begin with), but had never experienced. For the rest of the day, I did not obsess about food as I normally did. Food thoughts did not distract me from concentrating on schoolwork.

Let me repeat that:

*For the first time in my life, I did not obsess about food, and food thoughts did not distract me from concentrating on schoolwork.*

I have since then, developed this into a self-awareness process technique called "Food Meditation." There are two ways to do the food meditation. If you tend to be the type who binges, eating large amounts of food after a period of restriction, you will want to do the "Planned Binge" along with the food meditation. This means that you will buy twice the amount of food that you think you can eat. On the other hand, if you just eat too much at a meal or have any other type of food issue, you will want to do the food meditation without the planned binge. This includes an exercise to heighten your awareness of your food experience.

The first step is to write a list of all the foods you love. Include food that you love to eat but feel that you should not indulge in. If you tend to go for the cookies and ice cream, use these for your food meditation. If you enjoy fats such as fried foods, put these on your list. Do not stop at that. Think carefully about all those foods that you wish you could eat. Yes, the ones you lecture yourself that you should not be eating. If you could eat anything you really wanted without gaining weight, what foods would you reach for? Those are the ones you'll list.

Next, plan a time in which you will buy all of these delicacies. For those who tend to restrict eating and then binge, it is important to buy twice the amount of food you think you can eat in one sitting. The reason for this is simple: You need to test your limits. You need to let yourself find the point of satisfaction. Even if the point at which you are gratified is with more food than your body actually needs, at least we have a place to begin. You can always learn to develop contentment with less food later. This is called a planned binge. However, if your food issues are different, just do the food meditation exercise (see page 168).

When you berate yourself for eating, you cut yourself off from the experience of satisfaction. Satisfaction is the point at which you feel you have had enough. This feeling creates a natural desire to stop eating. Therefore, it is imperative to let go of judgments and choose an environment where you can let down your guard.

A note of caution: Many people will resist this exercise. One 300-pound client complained that she would eat an entire cake in one sitting. When I told her to buy two cakes for her food meditation, she insisted that this would lead to further binge eating. My response was this: "You've been bingeing for all these years. I know from experience that this will not have this effect. But let's say you are right. One more week of doing something you've been doing all along can't hurt you any more than you've been hurting yourself." She finally agreed to do the process and found a great deal of success in stopping her old destructive eating patterns.

All of my clients who come to me to change eating patterns do this process. Here are some responses:

- "I was at the grocery store the day after I did the Food Meditation. A clerk was handing out samples. I automatically responded in my old way by grabbing for one and shoved it quickly into my mouth. A moment later, as if struck by a bolt of awareness, I stopped and paid attention to the food in my mouth. It was pasta. It felt cold on my tongue. I didn't care for the flavoring. I realized I really didn't want it. In the past, I would have swallowed it long before I'd had a chance to notice the taste and texture. This time, I actually spit it out into the trash. I didn't like it, and I finally knew that I did not have to have it. I had a choice about it. This was an incredible miracle."
- Another had this to say: "I always thought I enjoyed food. I figured that was the reason I couldn't stop eating. After I did the food meditation exercise, I learned that it was the escape into food that took me away from my problems that I was enjoying. I did not know how to enjoy the food itself. I find that I now refuse to eat unless I can sit down and take the time for the pleasure of it. I no longer eat on the run. If I don't have time for a meal, I'll wait until I do. If I'm really hungry but can't afford the time for a regular meal, I'll take a couple of minutes for a nutritious snack to tide me

> over. Eating on the run is no longer an option. Not only do I feel better about my eating pattern, but my car is cleaner too. I no longer have a stash of wrappings from fast food restaurants."

Once you have developed eating awareness, you will begin to make choices about what food you want and when. It is only when you give yourself permission to make any choice that you will be free to make a choice not to eat it. This includes choices about when you eat and what type of food (even if it is food that is not healthy for you). To get to this point, it is imperative that you give yourself several weeks to several months of "awareness eating" without restraint as to the portion size or the type of food.

If you desire fast food, see to it that you choose it. Remember only one guideline is in place at this stage. You can eat as much as you want, whatever type of food you want, at any time that you want, as long as you are awake and conscious when you eat. It is imperative at this stage of learning intuitive eating that you disregard any knowledge about what foods are healthy or the calorie or fat content. Choose each food according to the signals of your body. When making choices, also consider what you want to eat. Later, I will show you how to incorporate healthy eating without threatening a rebellion from your natural desires.

## *Body Talk*

During a hypnotherapy session with Jim, I gave suggestions that he pay attention to his body and its desires and needs. I helped him to understand the difference between what his stomach wanted and his mouth or any other part of his body. When he opened his eyes, he said that his mind was telling him to go get Taco Bell Mexican food. I asked him to check in with his stomach. He noticed his stomach felt comfortable.

> *I suggested he tell his mind that his stomach wasn't ready for food. Ask if it would be willing to wait until his stomach was hungry? His eyes opened wide with surprise and he said, "The drive to eat is going away!"*

I told him to close his eyes and talk to his mind. I suggested he negotiate with the part of him that wanted the Mexican food. I suggested he tell it that his stomach wasn't quite ready for food. Tell it he would be willing to give it Mexican food a little later if it would wait until his stomach was ready. Within one minute of self-talk, his eyes opened wide with surprise and he said, "It's going away!"

When you honor different parts of yourself and treat each part with respect, you will get far more cooperation than if you coerce yourself. When you go on a diet, one part of you attempts to overpower another. When part of you is sick of being bullied into restrictive eating, it rebels. This is one reason why you feel out of control after a diet. Each of these parts in essence has its own mind.

If you and a friend each wanted to eat at a different restaurant, you wouldn't shout at each other. You wouldn't say, "I'm going to get my way no matter what you want."

Instead, you would negotiate. You might make an agreement to eat at one restaurant this time and the other one next time. It's much the same with your body.

The next time you want to eat, ask yourself what you want. Let's say you want a hamburger. Then pay attention to your stomach. Ask it if it's hungry and if it also wants a hamburger. If it does, then by all means, go ahead and eat it. If it doesn't, then ask what part of you wants the hamburger. Perhaps it's your mouth or your mind. Then begin the negotiations. The "Talking Parts" exercise guide you through a conversation with your body.

### *Intuition and Nutrition*

Throughout my childhood and well into my adulthood, I suffered from an insatiable craving for sweets. It was so bad that I isolated myself. I could barely function well enough to be around people. I could not count on how long I could go without this uncontrollable need to eat sweets. I wouldn't eat in front of others because I was riddled with shame. It led to a life of extreme loneliness. When I was with friends, I wanted to leave so I could eat. When I was eating, I wished I could stop so I could enjoy being with friends.

One day I heard about an eating plan that would eliminate sweet cravings. It took me a while to work up to making the commitment to try it for a period of time. It was restrictive. I'd always been against restrictions that would send me flying in the opposite

> ***After a short period of time, I had absolutely no physical cravings for sweets.***

direction, but I finally decided to try it for thirty days anyway. I knew I could change my mind at any time if I wanted to. I approached it as an experiment; something I could learn about. It was astonishing. After a short period of time sticking to the plan, I had absolutely no physical cravings for sweets. Let me say that again: I HAD ABSOLUTELY NO PHYSICAL CRAVINGS FOR SWEETS.

I knew my answer was somewhere in this experience. Yet, I missed the sweets in my mind. I remembered how I had enjoyed them in the past although I did not feel any physical need for them after my 30-day experiment. I felt that I could not emotionally make the commitment to eat this way for the rest of my life. Yet I discovered after I fulfilled my 30-day commitment and went on to earlier unhealthy habits of eating sweets, I craved to go back to the more nutritious and satisfying foods.

I then decided to eat in this way just one particular meal or one particular day at a time. After a while, I noticed I was seeking out this healthier type of food from my 30-day experiment more often. Because I re-educated my body in a gentle process, it responded to the true need to eat healthy foods. That eating plan is now the basis for 90 percent of my food choices. I can honestly say I eat in a healthy way overall. I have integrated this into my everyday life. (I followed a plan that suggested more protein and very few carbohydrates. The basic premise is that people who crave sweets need to eat more protein and eliminate all refined carbohydrates. My plan recommends about twice the protein

***Because I re-educated my body in a gentle process, it responded to the true need to eat healthy foods.***

than the Weight Watchers' diet. No wonder why the Weight Watchers diet never worked for me—I truly walked around hungry all the time.)

Has this 90 percent healthy eating led me to a skinny body? No. It has led me to a life of emotional and physical health. I am resigned. I will never meet that illusive American ideal body image. If I can't be thin, I am determined to become as attractive as my "perfectly imperfect" shape and size will allow. I've noticed that a fit body is an attractive body. I have decided to be as fit as I can be. I don't let excess fat stop me from this. I focus in on what I can do, not what I can't do. Some of my clients have found this approach to help them lose weight without yo-yo-ing.

We have allowed science to dictate how much food and what type is good for us and when we should eat it. "Don't eat after 6:00, and you'll lose weight." Dr. Atkins says to eat mostly protein, avoid carbohydrates, and you'll lose weight. Another scientific theory says to eat protein and carbohydrates in equal amounts and at each meal. The food-combining plan dictates not to combine carbohydrates with proteins.

Doesn't it just make you want to scream? All of this scientific evidence showing us how to be thin has created a nation of fat people. Isn't it possible that all of this analysis, all of this "proof" is wrong? We are looking in the wrong place.

Where else can we look for answers? When in doubt, I like to find answers in their most natural form: in nature. Once it was natural to eat food when you were hungry and to stop when you'd been satisfied. We're so out of touch with what that all means. So how do we get back to it?

Food knowledge you have developed through the years will guide you unconsciously. (If you do not have basic nutritional information, begin now to develop some. An excellent resource is the book, "Your Fat Is Not Your Fault" [see Resources section]. This approach is the most sensible one I've seen, and it is quite individualized.) It works like the information you put in your brain about how to drive from one place to another. Once you know the directions, you can let go of the conscious and deliberate need to keep it at the forefront of your mind. You trust you will know where to turn and when. In much the same way, once you experiment with food amounts, appropriate times of the day to eat, and what types of food you eat, you will become automatic in your response to the very basic need of eating. Good self-esteem is at the basis in order to trust yourself to do this right. You must accept your body as it is, at least for now. The drive to look a certain way interferes in the natural process, and listening to your body will help you to make better choices. Change your eating habits first. Changing your body will come later. The Food Exercises, The Paradox, and Food Meditation will help you understand food cravings compared to choices.

### *A Word About Commitment*

A diet commitment requires extreme willpower. The type of commitment you will learn to use here is a gradual one that will feel natural. The strong "discipline" that keeps failing you is not required. The type of commitment I'm suggesting here is a process of commitment.

First, you will make a commitment for one day or one meal. Then you free up your choices to include all foods. Then you isolate another day or another single meal and make the commitment for that. This second time becomes easier to do because you are now motivated. You remember the rewards, the good feeling from a previous time. You will find, over time, your desire to eat food that is more nutritious occurs more often. Yet you are still free to choose less than nutritious foods without feeling guilty or that you "blew it." The "Behavior Experiment" exercise will help you to make these gradual changes.

Like braiding different strands together, slowly interweaving changes with your existing eating patterns will help you make the changes a part of you. This process works far better than the disruptive "on-and-off-the-diet" pattern.

### *A Side Tip*

Suppose you've been experimenting with foods and patterns that make you feel good. Perhaps you remember how good you felt when you ate the more nutritious foods, but your taste buds tell you they want something sweet now. Try telling yourself that you will eat the nutritious food first. If after that you still desire the sweet thing, you will let yourself have it.

This serves two purposes. First, it will give your body a chance to get the nutrition it needs. Often, the need for the sweet will either disappear or be reduced after your basic hunger is satisfied. You will find that you can satisfy the need for something sweet with a smaller amount once the nutritional needs are satisfied. It will also help you change your behavior without threatening deprivation. Without the feeling of deprivation, you feel no need to overcompensate, and the overindulgence reaction will not occur.

### *Cause and Effect*

I remember in my early twenties I changed my early morning sugar habit. It was then that I started to notice a bad feeling in my stomach when I ate sugar first thing in the morning. By then, I was already using some of these techniques, and it was extremely easy to make this particular change.

I concentrated intensely on the behavior and its associated consequences. I noticed the pain in my stomach and the drain of physical and mental energy afterwards. (I didn't know then, but I was probably experiencing low blood sugar). To myself I loudly stated, "I notice when I eat this Danish on an empty stomach, I feel pain in my stomach. I also notice I feel drained and tired all morning." By saying this out loud, it forced me to acknowledge what I was actually doing. After a while, I couldn't deny it. In addition, I was able to make a connection between cause and effect. My behavior caused the effect. I forced myself to pay attention to this truth. Because I was awake and conscious, I changed the behavior without judgment about it. Within two or three days, I totally eliminated it. I have never gone back to sugar in the morning and never struggled with that particular eating pattern again.

One way to change behavior patterns is to become hyper-aware of the consequences of that behavior. It is imperative to do this without judgment.

- Notice the behavior and the associated consequence. Do this without judgment.
- Allow yourself to continue the behavior and make a conscious choice to continue it.
- Continue to make the choice until a light bulb goes off in your brain. You will know when this happens because you will acknowledge that if you can make a choice to do this behavior, you can also make a choice not to do this behavior. For some things, it may take months; for other things, awareness comes sooner. This can only happen when you make the connection with being at the level of choice about this, not when you are a victim of the compulsion.
- Remember, you can only get to the level of choice when you are aware and conscious about your choice. You can only experience this when you are free of judgments.

Marcie was an emotional eater. She let her feelings dictate when and what to eat. With each emotional situation, she would avoid the problem and reach for food for comfort. If she and her husband had an argument, she would reach for chocolate cake. If she was dreading a doctor's appointment, she would call ice cream to the rescue. If she had an upcoming social event that meant she would have to face a closet full of clothes that wouldn't fit, she would convince herself chocolate candy would help her cope. Her problems seemed to disappear while indulging in eating. Then came the letdown.

First, she felt bad about the still unresolved situation. Next came her realization of how much she'd eaten. The guilt of having eaten inappropriately left her feeling empty and searching for something more.

Marcie was disgusted. She used some of the techniques in this book to change her behaviors, and this is what she said about the results: "It is so amazing to me. This was a life-long problem I feel like I have conquered. It [emotional eating] is no longer an issue in my life. I might have a craving for chocolate, and I will eat a square or two of chocolate. This is something that was beyond my thought process two months ago. I would never have thought not to eat the whole thing. Now I think, 'Okay, I've had my sweet tooth fulfilled. I'll just save the rest.' With my last two pregnancies, I gained over 60 pounds. With this pregnancy, I've gained only 10 pounds, and it was a lot healthier."

*"It's so amazing to me. Emotional eating is not longer an issue in my life."*

### *Food for Your Natural Size*

Once you have experimented with different types of foods and you find you are making healthful choices without forcing them on yourself, you are ready to set yourself up for body-size success. Here is where you will choose the types of foods in the amounts you need and at the right times of day to support the body size that is right for you.

The key here is to go for a physical goal without bringing back the obsessive thinking about food and your body.

In physics, water seeks its own level; a natural equilibrium. In much the same way, if you'll follow the wisdom of your body's messages, your body will find its natural and right size. The imagery exercise on page 176 will help you to engage your wisdom self.

### ***Brain Hiccups***

You may not always be able to identify the problem that prompted your impulse to eat. It just may be what I like to call a hiccup in the brain. Accept these unexplained reasons and do your best to choose a coping strategy. Sometimes you will eat when you are not hungry and do not feel entirely justified in using food as a crutch. Accept this too. The mysterious phenomenon is part of the way things are. The sooner you accept it, have compassion for yourself and get on with living, the better the chances that the impulse will not repeat itself.

When you resist certain forces, such as brain hiccups, they persist. Like the ocean waves, you cannot control them. Enjoy jumping through them, riding them back to shore, and just playing with the waves. If one catches you off guard, relax and let the wave take you for a ride. If you fight it, you will more than likely be tossed around. Which do you think would be more fun?

## Chapter 5—The Joy of Exercise:

# Fitness for Your Natural Size

*Don't be afraid of opposition. Remember, a kite rises against, not with, the wind.*

Hamilton Mabie

Have you ever heard: "Now dear, it's not that I don't like the way you look. You should lose weight for health reasons." Some well-doers disguise their prejudice about appearance with the concern for physical fitness.

How often I had been told that health should motivate me to squeeze myself into a size eight. However, at a size 18, I was able to run a mile in about 15 minutes. That is a respectable speed at any size. I was healthy, and this was proof.

Science even stepped in to back me up. I took an entire battery of medical tests that showed I was in excellent health. In fact, the assessment put my "health age" at 33—seven years younger than my chronological age. This means that my lung capacity, blood sugar level, and all those things that medical tests show, reflected someone

33 not 40. (Can't you just see me sticking my tongue out and saying "So there!")

Fitness began to work for me when I began to integrate simple and enjoyable body movement into my day-to-day life. When friends quit their rigorous exercise plans because they had exhausted themselves, I was learning how to pace myself. When I went through periods of inactivity, instead of forcing myself back to a dreaded routine like my friends who played the "all-or-nothing game," I gently reminded myself of the pleasures of physical activity. I became easily motivated because I was enticing myself, not "force feeding." I actually began to miss exercise. It no longer became something I had to talk myself into. I became internally motivated toward it. Even today I go through periods of inactivity. However, those times are less frequent. I can honestly say that exercise is part of my day-to-day life—not something I do for a few months during times of dieting and then recuperate from for the next year and a half.

> *I became easily motivated because I was enticing myself to exercise, not "force feeding."*

New government recommendations suggest more relaxed guidelines for exercise which affect longevity, general health, and risk of heart disease or stroke. More than a dozen studies support the efficacy of low-level daily activities such as walking, vacuuming, gardening, and the like. In addition, body movement activity does not have to be done at one time. You can garden for fifteen minutes in the morning and take a fifteen-minute walk after dinner and expect as good a level of improved fitness as if you'd exercised for thirty minutes at one time.

One benefit of body movement is its ability to decrease insulin levels. Increased insulin stimulates fat storage. Unlike dieting, exercise is one of the few things consistently associated with reducing body fat. In addition, it raises your metabolism.

Body movement is a natural need. Watch a child and the instinct to move can't be denied. Do we outgrow this basic necessity? Or does it become stifled and repressed with the demands of adulthood? Have you ever been bedridden for several days? Even after a day, do you notice the need to move around? If we start with the premise that motion is as much a driving force from within as the need to eat, you will see how to incorporate it into your life with as much ease as reaching for food when you're hungry.

If you didn't have to exercise, if you could be fit and healthy without it, what form of body movement would you naturally gravitate toward? Think you wouldn't want any exercise or movement at all? Try to be still for a period of time. Give yourself an assignment. For the next three weeks, from the time you come home from work until the time you go to bed at night you must sit on the couch. You are free to read or watch TV, but you cannot move from that spot. If you have a family, ask them to cooperate with this experiment. Ask them to prepare dinner and serve it to you on the couch. After a short time, notice a desire within you to walk, stretch, or make some other type of movement. If you can't do it for three weeks, do it for two full days on the weekend. You owe it to yourself to try. It will be quite enlightening.

You may interpret the need to move as something other than what it is. You may think what you want is to go shopping or some other type of activity that you don't correlate with movement. You may think you only want any type of change of scene. Would you be satisfied with sitting on a plane for ten hours or being taken for a day-long drive in a car after your sitting marathon? Probably not. Your body would be screaming out to move.

In Ripley's Believe it or Not Museum, one exhibit depicts a man confined to a jail cell so small that he could not stretch his full height either standing up or lying down. The thought of not being able to move around is so agitating to me, I couldn't bear to look at the exhibit for more than a quick moment without feeling extreme anxiety. Can you imagine a life without movement?

How can you capitalize on your natural inclination for movement? How can you utilize this basic need to motivate you toward your goal of health and fitness without exhausting yourself with unreasonable demands for exercise that lead you to burn-out?

You may want to begin with everyday movement to get you started. Here are some ideas:

- Unless you want to attach some weights to the ear piece and flex those biceps, leave the phone on the hook and walk to a neighbor's house instead of calling.
- Park your car at the far end of the store parking lot and walk, skip, hop, or run to get your shopping done. Make a game out of getting all your items as quickly as possible while race-walking through the aisles.

- When watching TV use each commercial as an opportunity to walk. Find a reason to get up and get an item in another room.
- Put household items you use frequently in hard-to-reach high places. Stretch your arms reaching for them. Or, put them in low places and squat down to get them.
- The ever famous walk the stairs instead of taking the elevator. Pretend you have claustrophobia and can't ride the elevator.
- Try to find something about movement that's enjoyable. Perhaps a morning stretch when you first wake up feels good to you. This is a start.

### *Exercise Patterns That Do Not Work*

How often I've heard people say that they exercise five or six times per week when they first decide to get off the couch and back into shape. When I've suggested that this is a bit excessive, their reply is inevitably the same. "No, you don't understand. It really feels good. I want to exercise this much. It doesn't feel forced at all."

Of course it doesn't at first. But what happens when you settle into the routine of it and the novelty wears off? The "high" that came from the start of something new that kept you motivated at first now feels like the humdrum of routine. To maintain that disciplined level of exercise usually results in burn-out. Because you cannot keep the pace, you usually end up back on the couch absorbed in TV and eating snacks every night. It doesn't happen all at once. It may take several weeks to deteriorate back to this total nonproductive state.

Typically, a person will miss one exercise session which seems reasonable. After all, you've been pretty good for the last month or two. The next day, you realize you are still tired, so you miss again. You promise yourself you'll get back on track tomorrow. But the next day you find you still cannot manage. You swear that you will really begin again next week. By the following week, you feel so bad about not having done what you were "supposed" to do that the negative attitude wears at you more. Again, you stay away from the gym. The spiral downward begins. You feel bad about yourself and your eating pattern starts to regress too.

Before you know it, you're back on the couch watching TV and munching away at snacks, barely aware of what you are doing. You stay in this mode until self-disgust prompts you to begin the pattern of rigorous exercise all over again. Does this "all or nothing" sound familiar?

Our society built this country on an obsessive-compulsive mind-set. We'll build and build and then when we're finished, we'll build some more. We become victims to our ambition. The very thing that was supposed to have set us free to enjoy life more has bound and gagged us. The treadmill has gone haywire and needs to be stopped. The key is to know the limitations and imperfections and allow for them before you begin the process.

*We became victims to our ambition. The very thing that was supposed to have set us free to enjoy life more, has bound and gagged us.*

### *Why These Patterns Don't Work*

When you buy a new car, it is exciting. You enjoy the newness. It takes you out of the routine of your day-to-day life to which you have become half-conscious. You may have been feeling half-alive and this re-awakens you. You become enthusiastic and might not even mind spending the money. After all, you're buying "happiness, aliveness, and fun." The same is true for exercise. At first, you are pleased to start something new. Finally, you are taking control of your life and that feels good too. The exercise itself stimulates the "feel good" brain chemicals and this too contributes to feeling eager.

After a while the car needs maintenance. Spending money for a tune-up or new tires provides no immediate gratification. The payments also trigger a feeling of drudgery. You hate digging into your pocket. You don't feel that you are buying happiness or fun the way you did when you first bought the car. Yet, you know this is necessary in order to continue to have a car in good working order. You fork out the money and do what you have to do. In much the same way, the zeal for exercise wears down.

Suppose you bought a car whose payments were well beyond your means. Eventually, you would have to give up the car. In much the same way, when you decide to exercise more than is right for you, you will not be able to maintain it.

Most people with the "all-or-nothing" pattern think that they must exercise five to six times per week for an hour or more each time. The media supports this mentality. In the 1960's, the entire country decided to get fit and

President Kennedy appointed a committee to lead us. Exercise physiologists studied, experimented, and researched our bodies. It was then that they determined that three times per week of twenty to thirty minutes is sufficient.

What happened to that research after the Kennedy era? The American philosophy, "more, bigger, better, and then some more," has taken over. We are a nation where "too much is not enough." We need bigger houses, better cars, more money-and still, we are not satisfied. Exercise is no exception.

Unless you want to be an athlete, a modest amount of exercise will do the job. What is the job you want to accomplish anyway? I know that when my body feels strong and fit, life is better. For me then, the goal is to be reasonably fit so that I am in the kind of shape that will support my enjoyment of life. In addition, I want to make sure that whatever illness I may develop, I am in good enough shape to recover as quickly as possible.

Of course I want the exercise to support my aliveness. Like food, it helps me enjoy life. I don't live to eat; I eat to live. In much the same way when you put exercise in perspective, it will support your life and not run your life. With this appropriate outlook, I can be successful in maintaining my goals over a long period. It is not something I do everyday for 3 months until I feel burned out and then recover from for the next year and a half.

Some people want to chase the rainbow. For them, these techniques will not work. Ask yourself what purpose does exercise serve? Do you want to use it only to get you to that illusive body size that you hope will make you magically happy? Has this worked for you in the past? Do you reach a certain goal and then give it all up? If this is true for you and you would like to try something different, here are my suggestions. The following pages explain "minimums and maximums." These have worked for me for many years. Although I may go through stages of exercising minimally, they are short-lived. I am back into my regular routine in no time. I have maintained this pattern for the long haul. Try the Fitness exercise in the Appendix to establish your own maximums and minimums, and see if they can work for you.

> ***When you put exercise in perspective, it will support your life, not run your life.***

### *Accepting Your Body's Limitations*

Women's bodies have limitations. How can we make these limitations work in our favor? When we do accept conditions that can't be changed, we are happier. So just what are these limitations?

The average woman is thirty percent fat. It's unrealistic to drop to twenty-two percent. Jazzercise instructors and women marathon runners who compete regularly, average eighteen percent (more if they are older than thirty). Women over thirty who run and train to compete have more than twenty-two percent fat. The team that climbed the Himalayas to altitudes over 18,000 feet was a tough group. The expectation was that their fat level would be low. Yet the average was twenty-one percent. Therefore, it is unlikely for the average women to measure under twenty-one to twenty-two percent fat.

Now here's the tough part to swallow, so I hope you're sitting down. At that percentage, fat jiggles! This is true even at eighteen percent fat. That's just the way it is. Nothing you can do about it. Since you can't fly, you've probably accepted that fact. I'll even bet you never think about it, let alone obsess about it. Is it possible that when you accept your limitations, you are more apt to relax and let go? Now try this with body fat: Invite the girls over to giggle, make some Jell-O, accept your own jiggle, and get on with enjoying life.

### *Too Much Is Not Enough*

Unless you are striving to be an athlete, a modest amount of exercise is all you need. Yet most Americans drag themselves off the couch only after a period of disgust with themselves. They arrive at the gym pumped and ready to tackle fitness as if they are entering the next iron-man competition. Within three months, burnout sends them back to the couch. What has happened? That American compulsive nature has taken over. The "too much is not enough" syndrome is driving us to the "all or nothing" mentality. Instead, incorporate moderation in exercise and maintain it over time. The key here is to sustain your exercise routine, not beat the rabbit to the illusive—and elusive—finish line of health.

### *Keeping Yourself Motivated*

A group of psychologists conducted an experiment to test motivation in toddlers. They asked moms to encourage their toddlers to throw a ball into the basket located on the other side of the room.

The task was beyond the ability of the children. Some mothers moved the basket closer to make it easier. Others insisted on telling their child to get the ball in the basket while it was still at the other end of the room. The ones who succeeded in getting the ball into the closer, easier basket were motivated to continue trying when the basket was then moved back to the far end of the room. The ones whose mothers insisted they throw the ball into the far-off basket lost their motivation and quit trying. Their failure killed their motivation.

Use this story to help you with your own motivation for success. Design an exercise plan which will help you feel a small sense of accomplishment. Then increase the challenge by small steps. Take the time to give yourself credit for each success along the way. Adjust your exercise plan to accommodate unexpected changes in your schedule. Allow for a minimum amount of acceptable exercise each week. Plan for a maximum amount of exercise. Make sure your maximum is realistic given the other demands of your life.

When you allow for a minimum number of times per week and a minimum number of minutes, you will set yourself up for success. Often, when people don't meet their expected routine, they give up. It becomes an all-or-nothing game. Instead, set the minimum so that no matter what else happens in your life, you are able to meet this small commitment.

Jonathan set a goal of a minimum of one time per week of 15 minutes of exercise. His maximum was three times per week for 30 minutes. He felt he could do more than this but I suggested he resist the temptation to exercise more. In the past he had pushed himself far more than he was ready for, and he set himself up for failure. Many times in the past he would exercise one hour or more each day, six days a week. Not surprisingly, he couldn't maintain it over the course of time.

I suggested he make the first goal to get a routine going. Fitness is not the first goal. To find a routine that you can maintain over time is foremost. Over the course of 6 months, he met every commitment. Several times he was only able to exercise once. But because he met his minimum obligation, he continued to feel good about himself.

In the past, he would expect himself to exercise 3-5 times per week for an hour each time. When he would fail to meet this demand, he felt bad about himself. One week he skipped a day or two. The next week, he'd remember his failure from the previous week and feel unmotivated again. He promised himself he'd get back on track the following week. Bet you can guess what happened the next week. This continued on, resulting in a complete breakdown of his exercise routine.

With this new minimum/maximum strategy, he was finally able to maintain an exercise pattern every week. The last time I spoke to him, he was three years into his commitment to himself. He continued with successful follow-through and eliminated his "all-or-nothing" failure pattern.

### *A Good Balance*

Once you have your minimum and maximum goals established, set about to find a good balance. Think of it this way. Over the course of a five-year period, you had periods in which you only reached your minimum goal, but because you met your minimum goal you were successful and were able to continue feeling good. Because you felt good about what you were doing, you continued with the maximum goals during other periods. Your overall exercise over five years was far more than had you done six times per week for two to three months. Let's chart this out. Imagine you began your program in September.

September 1-30, you exercised one time per week. You started to feel good, and you found more motivation and time. October 1-31, you exercised two times per week.

Then you had some additional demands on your life the first week in November, so you went back to one time per week during November 1-7. Things got better in the second week. You went back to two times per week for the rest of November.

Again in December, holiday demands left you with little time and energy, so you went back to one time each week. In January, you felt motivated to get your New Years resolution going so you bumped it up to three times per week. This lasted through March. Then the demands of getting your taxes together permitted time for only twice each week through the end of April.

Now with May and June yielding to summer, you felt more motivated to look good in your bathing suit, and you went back to three times per week. During summer, more outdoor activities counted as your exercise. The summer was easy.

Out of 12 months this first year, you exercised consistently throughout the year. With this pattern, you are likely to be far more healthy and slim than had you worked hard for three months and then quit. Imagine this flexible pattern over the course of 5 years. Wouldn't you be happier with yourself? I know that I am. (The chart on the next page shows how this works.)

- First, set a minimum amount of exercise.
- Fitness is not the first goal of exercise. Developing some success and a livable routine that can be maintained over time is the first goal.
- Next, set a maximum amount of exercise each week.
- Allow for the natural biorhythms of life. Accept the minimum and maximum routines as part of your overall pattern. Some weeks you will only do the minimum. Others you will do more.
- Notice how you are integrating a pattern of consistent exercise that you can maintain over the long haul.

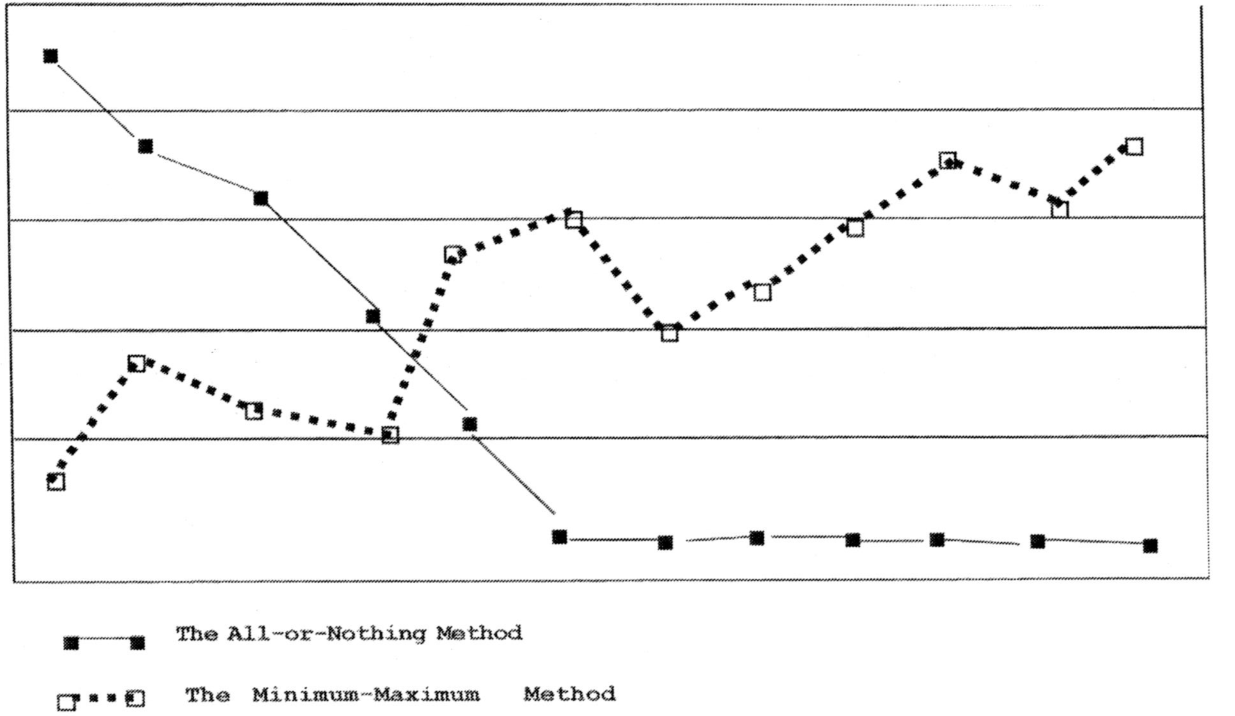
The All-or-Nothing Method
The Minimum-Maximum Method

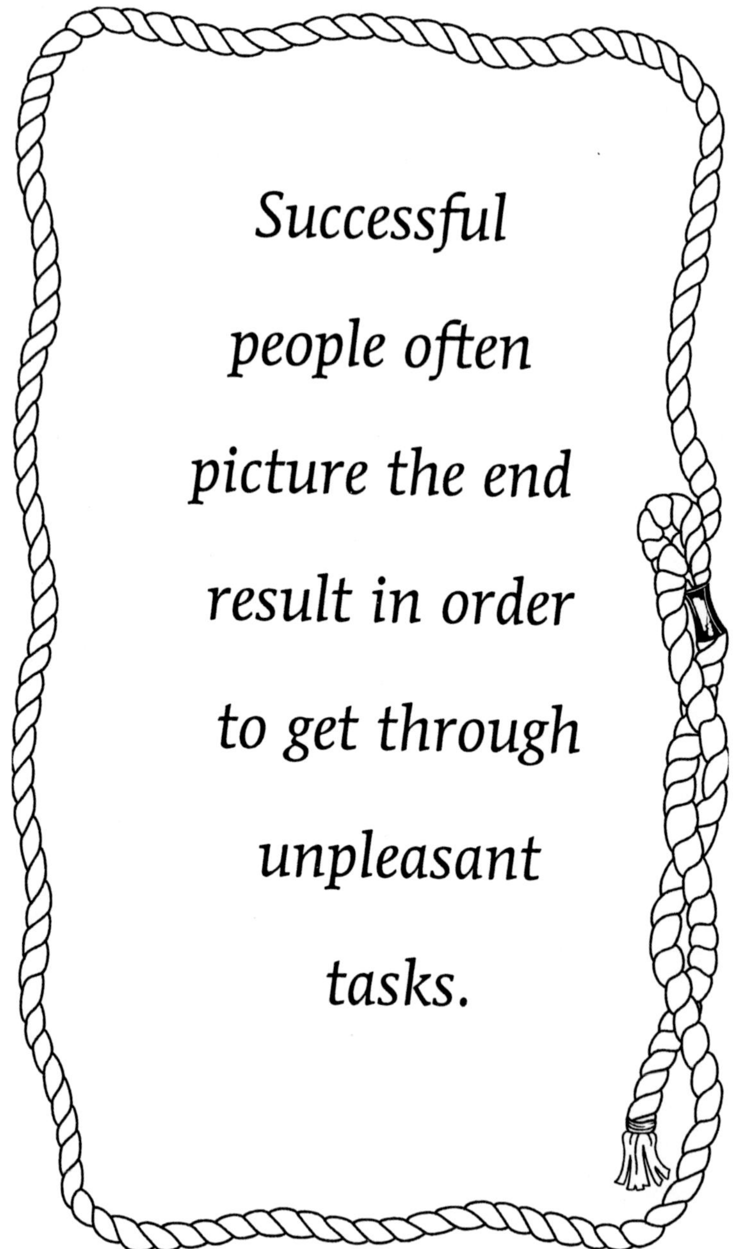

*Successful people often picture the end result in order to get through unpleasant tasks.*

**Chapter 6—Measuring Success:**

# Recognizing Your Achievements

Martha had a goal to run a 26-mile marathon, which was scheduled for May in Utah. She recently had a baby and was having trouble getting back into the athletic shape she'd been in before she was pregnant. I suggested a visual aid to keep her going. Each day she ran, she was to mark a map with the number of miles for that day as if she were running from her home in San Diego to Utah. She needed a total of 745 miles to complete the trip.

Her first day she ran ten miles. She drew a line to represent this distance on the map from her home toward her destination. Her first goal was to get past her 10-mile mental block. She had six months to finish her training. If she could increase her daily distance by two miles, maintain it for a week then go on to increase it by two miles the next week, it would take her two months to get to the 26-mile level she needed. Then she'd have four months to get comfortable at the 26-mile daily run. (This plan was realistic given the good shape she'd been in prior to her pregnancy.)

Each day her motivation was stronger because she could actually see her progress. Her first week, she ran 12 miles per day times 5 days per week, which totaled 60 miles. During her second week, she completed seventy miles. She drew a line on her map to represent 130 miles. She had just five hundred and fifteen miles to go, and she'd be in Utah. She displayed the map in her bedroom. From time to time, she'd glance at it and felt the inner stir to succeed. It also gave her confidence that she could make it.

By the time she had half the miles behind her, motivation was not a problem. In fact, she couldn't wait to get out to run each day.

When you devise mental tricks, your left brain stays interested in your pursuit. It will also serve as a distraction from any temporary discomfort you may experience during the exercise. Martha reported times when she felt her legs ache as she ran. She forced her mind to picture the map and the many miles she'd already accomplished. A surge of energy and motivation shot through her and distracted her from the painful moment.

While exercising, imagine the sense of accomplishment you will have when your exercise for that day is complete. Another motivator is to remember the good sense of well-being that you will feel.

### *A Friend That Betrays*

Like Brutus' fatal stab at Caesar, the bathroom scale is a friend that betrays. It takes you down the path of a distorted body image and can lead you to ultimate destruction. Many people who hate their bodies swear they have gained 5 pounds from last night's slice of pizza. What the scale does not show is that it is only temporary water retention that she usually gets when eating bread.

Women caught up in this unreliable means to determine success often end up feeling bad and gaining at the losing game. Defeatist attitudes lead to negative subjective feelings, you know, the ones that leave you feeling fat. You then end up with the attitude that says, "Oh heck, if I'm fat, and I feel so helpless to do anything, I might as well give in and eat everything in sight." This familiar mindset leads to the all-or-nothing mentality also known as the binge-diet behavior.

It seemed that every time I had attempted to lose weight, the scale either stayed the same or even inched up a bit. Talk about discouragement! Later, when I stopped dieting and took the holistic approach this book is based on, there were times when my clothes would feel bigger and I felt slimmer. Just out of curiosity, I'd get on the scale. Sure enough, the scale betrayed me again. I was either the same weight or a pound or two heavier. This time, however, armed with knowledge to combat the enemy, I stared the monster straight in the eyes.

Two things were working against this form of measurement. For one thing, I tend to make muscles easily, and muscle weighs more than fat. Therefore, since I'd been exercising, I knew the scale was measuring my muscle weight, and I had actually lost fat (as evidenced by my clothing). I'd taken a tape measure and measured each major area. Sure enough, I'd lost inches in most places except my thighs. I'd actually gained 1/4" of muscle. I knew it was muscle because my pants legs fit and my muscles actually bulged.

Another piece of the puzzle was knowing the body's need to maintain the status quo. Because of this, it will hold on to water. I noticed that while my clothes were definitely looser, I felt bloated. My body demonstrated its need to maintain its weight with water retention. Finally what I'd always known intellectually, I experienced: I kept my attitude in the right place and was able to maintain my good eating and exercise habits. Within a few weeks, the bloat was gone. Finally, the scale reflected the weight loss.

Imagine if I'd given up when I first noticed the water retention. People who get stuck on this unreliable measurement are cheating themselves. For one thing, if you are losing weight in an unhealthy way, you may be losing muscle weight or water weight. It may make you happy when you see it reflected on the scale. However, it is not the type of weight loss you want. For one thing, when you don't eat enough protein, you will lose muscle weight. You need muscle weight in order to continue to have a healthy metabolism. A healthy metabolism will continue to work off the calories you eat at a faster pace then an unhealthy weak one. In addition, fat weight is the type you want to lose. When you lose fat instead of muscle, you may weigh more, but you will fit into smaller size clothing. The inches you have lost will reflect a trimmer body than pounds on a scale.

The scale has finally taken a back seat in my life. I occasionally consider it, but I don't put much weight on it-literally and figuratively.

It's up to you. You can get the immediate gratification reflected on the scale from water or muscle loss that comes from unhealthy dieting. Or, you can draw on your maturity that wants the true weight loss from fat loss and a long-term commitment to lifestyle change.

I am the same clothing size now as I was when I weighed 20 pounds less. This phenomenon could have sent me into a spiral of negativity if I had been using the scale to measure my success. Since I am what they call a "muscle maker," I cannot expect to have the scale reflect true weight loss. I am delighted to experience my healthy body in appropriate-sized clothing when I know I am exercising moderately and eating well.

What then is a reliable means for measuring success? Your feelings are the least stable way to determine progress towards a goal. Some days feel better than others. When you feel bad, you are more likely to view yourself negatively. Don't trust "feelings" as a measure of success. Behavior is more objective and is more within the control of the individual. Try "goal-supporting behaviors" as a measure of success and save those subjective "feelings" for the next romance novel.

> ***Don't trust feelings as a measure of success. Use goal-supporting behavior and leave those subjective feelings for the next romance novel.***

Objective measurements are necessary in order to know if you have reached a goal. Also, to reach a goal, it must be one that is within your control. For example, you would not make a goal to win a million dollars. This is more of a dream or a vision. You do not have control over this. However, you could set a goal to buy 10 lottery tickets each week in an effort to reach your dream.

In much the same way, trying to control weight via the scale involves too many unknown variables. For example, water retention and your body's resistance to change affect the scale. In addition, science has yet to figure out other unknown variables.

If we knew all the elements that controlled weight, the many people who have put in sincere effort to weigh less would have succeeded or at least some of us would have by now. The fact that we, as a nation, weigh more than ever before despite our attempts to diet should tell us something.

Instead of that magical number on a scale, create goals based on behavior that give you a sense of control. You can decide the number of times each week you exercise. In addition, you have power over the number of healthful meals you choose.

*Instead of that magical number on the bathroom scale, create goals based on behavior that give you a sense of control.*

### *Fail-Safe Patterns*

When one falls short of a goal, it usually affects self-esteem. People who do not have confidence usually set very high expectations for themselves. Because these unrealistically high expectations cannot be met, the individual usually falls short of the goal. Because they fall short, their need to attain even higher success becomes stronger. It is as if these extraordinary achievements will compensate for the inferior feelings. Of course, they cannot reach those unreasonable goals, so they fall short again. Once again, higher expectations and the cycle continues. With this in mind, the following pattern is designed to maintain success under all circumstances. It is almost fail-safe.

### *The Tiger at your heels...*<br>*Or the Carrot out in front of you...*

Melissa said, "I can't stand the way I feel any more, I'm willing to do anything to stop the dragged-out tired feeling." Melissa motivated herself with negativity. She was in pain and wanted to get away from it. She moved away from what she did not want.

In contrast, Meagan formulated her goal in terms of things she wanted rather than things she did not want. "I want to feel good. I want the energy to do the things I enjoy doing." Meagan motivated herself toward what she did want.

Either motivation style will work but you need to understand what method lights your own fire. To find out, ask yourself to define your goal. If you find yourself stating what you don't want, you "go away from" or are negatively motivated. If you state your goal in terms of what you do want, then you "go toward" or are positively motivated.

The Tiger at Your Heels... or the Carrot in Front? It is crucial to keep your motivation in the forefront of your mind. If you are going for the carrot, always keep it in front of you. If you are going to go the other way, always keep the tiger chasing at your heels.

Melissa fell into a short-lived motivation trap. After several weeks of exercise, she started to feel better. Because she succeeded in getting rid of that which she didn't want, she accomplished her goal. She was no longer in pain, lost her reason for continuing, and quit exercising. She didn't realize she was setting herself up for this. Her goal was to get out of pain and she accomplished this. It would have been better to set a goal that included a time frame.

*Keep the tiger at your heels, or the carrot out in front of you.*

For example, she might have said, "I want to get out of this sluggishness and stay away from that feeling for a year." The next time she wanted to get off her exercise plan, she could remind herself about how tired she had been. Stopping would lead her right back. This is keeping the tiger at your heels. The same thing is true for those who are motivated toward something. Here's a formula for success:

- Allow for a minimum of acceptable exercise each week.
- Plan for a maximum amount of exercise.
- Decide if you are motivated by:
- Going toward what you want, or
- Away from what you don't want
- If you are going for the carrot, always keep it in front of you.
- If you are going away from, always keep the tiger chasing you from behind.
-

## *All or Nothing*

Goal-supporting behavior means that you put your focus on the behavior rather than on the results. If you meet the behavior requirements, you have succeeded.

You may remember Evil Knievel and his daredevil motorcycle stunts. His son Robbie, followed in his footsteps. One day before a dangerous stunt, a reporter asked him what he was going to do with the million dollars he would win if he succeeded. He said he wouldn't allow himself to focus on the money because it would distract him from his goal.

Robbie's mind was focused on his behavior, and his reply showed this. He knew he could control his actions. He also knew he could not control the results of his behavior. Therefore, he could not allow himself to think of the money because that was beyond his control. If he allowed himself to think of the money, it would distract him from the task. He would then lose his focus, which was riding his motorcycle over the stretch of cars. This lack of focus would increase his chances of failure. In his case, a failure could likely be the end of his life.

The poem on the next page drives this point home.

## *Winning the Slim Body:*
*The Ultimate Distraction*

In much the same way, the gold is for the archer, holding out the slim body as the reward, drains you of power. It becomes a false friend.

## THE NEED TO WIN

by Chuang Tzu

When an archer is shooting for nothing
    He has all his skill.
    If he shoots for a brass buckle
    He is already nervous.
    If he shoots for a prize of gold
    He goes blind
    Or sees two targets—
    He is out of his mind!
His skill has not changed. But the prize
    Divides him. He cares.
    He thinks more of winning
    Than of shooting—
    And the need to win
Drains him of power.

Diet mentality inevitably results in its opposite. Excessive eating follows restrictive eating. Because of this, it is important to measure your eating style in some other way.

The diet mind-set usually sets dieters up for expecting perfect adherence. Being perfect is not possible, but most people try anyway. Failure to be perfect leads to frustration, which causes the dieters to abandon the diet. Then, knowing only rigid eating or binge eating, they resort to binge eating. This "all-or-nothing mind-set" is the roller coaster of dieting or "yo-yo" eating.

In addition to psychological reasons for failing at dieting, physiological reasons contribute. Research shows that brain chemicals rebel against drastic changes in sugar and fat intake. According to Elliott Blass, Ph.D., at Cornell University, links exist between cravings for sweet and creamy foods and the brain's morphine-like chemicals that produce pleasurable feelings. Blass speculates that when people attempt restrictive diets or reduce their fat or sugar intake too quickly, they might trigger these appetite-regulating brain chemicals and throw them into a state of chaos. Thus, in an attempt to correct this, the dieter swings from abstinence to binge eating. This research suggests that it may not be a matter of willpower at all. Even the most reasonable of diets may trigger these chemical responses.

***It may not be a matter of willpower at all. Even reasonable diets may trigger chemical responses in the brain that drives the dieter to overeat!***

*Measure Food* Behavior

To avoid the diet mind-set, first categorize your meals into four different groups: "Optimal, reasonably good, not great but not bad, and total OOPS!" Since all diet dropouts have had nutritional training from each diet they've tried, apply that knowledge to the four categories.

This book is not meant to be a nutritional guide. It is meant to be more of a behavior guide and an attitude guide. If you need more nutritional information, the bookstores are loaded with books to help you. In addition, the Weight Watchers diet, the American Heart Association diet, the Carbohydrate Addict's Diet are all good ones. You might want to read the Feel Good diet as recommended by Elizabeth Somer in her book, "Food and Mood:

The Complete Guide to Eating Well and Feeling Your Best." It has some excellent eating plans. The "Serotonin Solution," by Judith J. Wurtman, suggests more carbohydrates to help balance the brain chemicals.

Choose a plan that fits your needs. Remember, you are about to go through a process of experimentation. It does not matter what plan you choose, you will not be using it as a diet. You will get in touch with the effect different foods have on you. You will notice which satisfy you and which do not. Then you can come to your own conclusion as to what foods are right for you. Selecting a plan gives you a place from which to begin.

### *Guidelines not Rigid Rules*

Then, classify meals in each of the four categories. An optimal meal would fit perfectly with your chosen eating plan. For example, a dinner might include; small baked potato, salad with a tablespoon of dressing, 3 ounces of chicken breast, and a half-cup of vegetables. Remember, this is the optimal meal, not one that you will choose each time.

The next classification is "reasonably good." This is a meal that meets your chosen eating plan's overall idea of good nutrition, although it does not perfectly meet its guidelines. For example, it may include a little extra butter, a larger baked potato, a chicken sandwich with some type of sauce on the bread, and a medium frozen yogurt.

The next category might include a few foods in the plan, but more foods that are not good sound nutrition. It might be a slightly bigger portion or it might include some foods that have too many carbohydrates, sugars, or fats.

You might call this meal "not so great but not so bad."' After all, it does have some healthy nutrition in it. However, its downfall is that it provides too many calories. Remember, the goal here is a healthy body. It is not a predetermined number on a scale that fits with your idealized image of yourself.

Then suppose you eat a meal of fast food, or one that has little nutrition, or one that might have some nutrition but has far too much fat or sugars. This might be called "total OOPS."

*The 80/20 Rule*

If you eat "optimal" or "reasonably well" 80 percent of the time, you need not concern yourself with the other twenty percent. Let's say a person chooses a pattern of eating that includes three small meals and three snacks each day. Multiply six eating opportunities times seven days per week and you have 42 opportunities for food choices.

To follow the 80/20 rule, you would make sure that 33 of those chances met the "optimal" or "reasonably good" classification. The other nine occasions may fall into the "not so great" or "total OOPS." In fact, I often tell my clients to make sure at least 10% of their choices fit into the latter two categories.

This serves several purposes. The first thing it does is to satisfy your desire to have these other foods, which prevents a feeling of deprivation. It also helps you to know that if you do want these foods you can have them. That itself often releases the desire for them. It is often that which is forbidden that leads to temptation. Now that nothing is forbidden, nothing fuels the temptation. If it is truly okay to eat ice cream, and in fact, expected that you should eat it sometimes, you will be more inclined to become aware of what you truly want to eat at a given moment rather than what you should eat. You will find, more often than not, the good food is something you truly want anyway.

At first, you will probably not meet the 80 percent guideline. If you are honest with your true food desires, you will go through a period of testing what you actually want.

### *Your True Desire*

It is imperative that you first explore and examine your desires. In my private practice, I recommend that each client go through at least a week or two without regard to whether they are choosing healthy food or not. I direct them to experiment with their true desire and choice each time they select food.

To help you identify your experience use two of the four following sentences during this process; I want, I don't want, I choose and I choose not. Ask yourself if this particular food is what you really want or if it is out of habit. If you are beginning this process after a period of bingeing or not eating well, you will more than likely want more junk food than healthy food at this stage of the game. This is because you have gone on "automatic pilot." You automatically reach for junk foods because it is easier. During this part of the process, it is expected that you will want and choose foods that are not good for you. This is OK as long as you are making a conscious choice.

Throughout this process, you will use two of the above sentences that apply to your experience of the food you select. It works like this. Let's say you have reached for a fast food hamburger and fries, as has been your typical habit. Before you eat it, ask yourself if this is what you truly want to eat right now. Let's suppose the answer is yes. Next find the "choice" based sentence that applies: "I choose to eat this hamburger and fries." Now you have raised the level of awareness. You have begun to make a choice about something (see the "Stop Shoulding on Yourself exercises).

The compulsion or automatic response becomes something within your control. You are no longer a victim to the response, but are making a choice about it. This is an excellent first step. Go ahead and eat your chosen food without guilt, judgment, or shame.

In this beginning stage, I often have to convince clients not to judge this choice. If you judge it, you will cut yourself off from the experience of eating it, which will defeat the purpose. Your bad feelings will make you "go unconscious" so you don't have to face what you are doing. This is how a compulsion is developed. A compulsion is defined as an "uncontrollable need to do an irrational act." You may have experienced a compulsion after a period of restrictive eating. You feel out of control. This technique can help give you back your control.

Marge continually told herself she was stupid for choosing fried food when she wanted to be healthier. It is true that she was not making a choice that was consistent with her goal. But she certainly was not stupid. By finally awaking to the realization that her choice was at odds with her goal, she was no longer a victim to the "automatic pilot" reaction. She was able to accept the fact that her behavior was inconsistent. It was a truth, not a crime.

She noticed she made this inconsistent choice repeatedly. Each time she chose fast foods, she would say aloud to herself, "I want this and I choose it." Once she did this many times, she finally became aware of the ability to make a choice to not have the greasy food. If she was in fact choosing it, as her statement was verifying, then she had the ability to make a different choice. The next time she wanted fast foods, she found herself saying, "I want this and I choose not to have it."

Please note that it is often necessary to make the conscious choice to carry out the negative behavior many times before you become capable of experiencing the ability to change your choice. Each time you repeat the statement, "I want and I choose," you become more aware. A part of you wants to deny the reality of your choice. It seems that a strong knock on the head with a hammer is needed. It is a stubborn part of yourself and will only respond when it is being forced to open its eyes. Only then will it really see what it is doing.

After Marge selected to not have it, she could make a different decision later. She could choose it. It was not a matter of giving it up forever or for the length of the diet. She could choose it another time as long as it was within the twenty percent of her eating choices. After several days of selecting healthier foods, she then began to desire more healthy foods.

### *Making Choices*

The next step during this self-examination stage is to isolate a few days in which you will choose only healthy foods. Each time you select these nutritious foods, notice how you feel. Do you have more energy? Does the food sustain you over a longer period? Create as much awareness around this experience as you can. Talk aloud to yourself. You might want to write down what you ate and how filling or satisfying it felt.

At first, the two sentences which may apply here would be, "I don't want this food" and "I choose it anyway." Because you have been accustomed to eating junk food, the nutritious food may not appeal to you until you have re-introduced it to your taste buds. Remember, unlike a diet, you can make a different choice the next meal or the next day. This is a gradual process of changing your eating pattern, not an overnight miracle change.

As I stated previously, when I tried my thirty-day plan to deal with cravings for sweets, I made the commitment for only that period of time. Over the course of the next several years, I found that I desired to eat more frequently in the way that made me feel good. Because I was not in a hurry to make this change, I was able to interweave it into my life in a natural and easy way. When I have short periods of eating too much junk food, I can honestly say that I crave to get back to my better eating pattern. I miss the good food more than I used to miss the unhealthy food. I am now able to sustain

> ***I have finally done what "diets" claim that you should do... make it a lifestyle.***

the good eating habit over longer periods without any feeling of deprivation. I have finally done what "diets" claim that you should do...made it a lifestyle.

*Goal-Supporting Behavior*

The next goal then, is to reach 80 percent or 33 opportunities for good eating. (This is assuming three small meals and a 3-snack pattern of eating.) Once you achieve this, the goal is to maintain that level of eating over a period of one month, then two months etc. Now you are measuring your success by your behavior (which is in your control), and not by the unpredictable number on the scale or that illusive thing we call slim or that subjective feeling of being the right size.

When you go on a diet, it is usually because you feel flawed. This is a position of weakness. Instead, put yourself in charge with this outlined measuring style. Give yourself checks and balances and prevent that "all-or-nothing" mind-set. Allow for imperfections without the associated feelings of guilt. This, along with the earlier exercise measurement technique, will help you feel successful. Success feelings promote more success, and you build from a position of strength. To build from a positive position is empowering.

## Chapter 7—Relaxation:

# The Key to Losing Body Fat

*Men are disturbed not by things, but by the view which they take of them.*

Epictetus, a Greek philosopher

Enter, the rat race! The demands to produce more, bigger, and better stuff keeps us working sometimes through the night and often on weekends. You can get a caffeine jolt or sugar energy burst from your nearest 7-11 at noon or three in the morning. Our hectic pace accounts for a prescription for Prozac written every 30 seconds in the United States. (You know I'm exaggerating, don't you?) Do you think all this medication and over-indulgence would be necessary if we slowed down a bit and relaxed?

*Imagine Deputy Barney Fife sitting on the porch in Mayberry. He leans back in his chair and says "Yep, Andy, I've gotta go down to the Doc and pick up my prescription for Prozac." Aunt Bea pushes the screen door open holding a pitcher of lemonade*

> *and says, "Oh that reminds me, Andy. Don't forget to bring Opie his Ritalin while he's down at the fishing pond or he'll be so hyperactive, he'll never be able to concentrate on catching a fish."*

Disappointments and problems appear magnified when you are tense, tired, or stressed. The common American outlet for this stress is an overindulgence in food and passive inactivity. These are destructive patterns that lead to obesity and negative attitudes.

I remember a time when people relaxed and spent time together doing nothing in particular except enjoying one another's company. Stores closed at 6 o'clock in the evening and all day on Sunday. People took Sunday drives to be with relatives and friends.

When was the last time you were relaxed? Not on vacation, when it's easy to leave tension behind. I'm talking about relaxed in your day-to-day life. A calm, confident feeling that you could make that deadline or fulfill those personal responsibilities without stressing about them.

Do you wish you had more time to relax but think it's a luxury you can't afford? Think again. Negative stress affects your metabolic rate, which reduces your body's efficiency to work off calories. Stress is even linked to gaining abdominal body fat.

Negative stress kills brain cells by preventing glucose (the brain's food) from entering the cells. Overeating and stress are linked. If your body is not metabolizing food properly because of stress, you may find yourself reaching for more food in an effort to compensate.

Dieting causes stress. The key then, is not to go on a diet, but to learn to handle stress. You will then naturally reduce your intake of unnecessary calories.

### *Stress Makes Your Body Struggle*

Stress in the human body is like rust on a machine. The machine works harder to produce when it is rusty than when it is well oiled. Relaxation helps the body and brain work smoothly in much the same way oil lubricates a machine.

Stress triggers 1500 different brain messenger chemicals from the hypothalamus and hormones from the pituitary gland and adrenal glands. Nerve impulses stimulate adrenals to produce adrenaline and cortisol. These hormones surge into blood stream. Excess adrenaline and cortisol raise blood pressure. Adrenaline increases the blood-clotting elements that narrow arteries and ultimately clog them. Over time, excess adrenaline and cortisol bombard the walls of the arteries, leaving places in the blood for fats to lodge. Excess adrenaline can also over-contract and rupture heart muscle fibers, weakening them and making them vulnerable to an electrical short-circuit. Excess cortisol can raise cholesterol, which contributes to hardening of the arteries.

Some scientist believe that 70 percent of all illness is stress related—from heart attacks to asthma to skin disorders to cancer. Stress also contributes to behaviors that contribute to illness, such as overeating, smoking, and inactivity. Relaxation is simply a necessity!

In a Harvard study, people who coped poorly with stress became ill four times more often than those with good coping styles. You've probably noticed in your own life that you reach for food more when you are stressed.

### *Five Minutes for Fun: Find Freedom From Fat*

If I could guarantee you could reduce your cravings for sweets by 50% and reduce your appetite by 25% just by spending 5 minutes twice a day doing a relaxation technique, would you do it? If my guarantee included increased health and the ability to run up the stairs like you did as a kid, just by spending 5 minutes a day would you do it? In 5 minutes once or twice a day, you can:

- Reduce or eliminate emotional eating.
- Reduce or eliminate cravings for specific foods such as sweets.
- Reduce your appetite.
- Metabolize food more efficiently and require less to be satisfied.
- Stay calm under pressure.
- Increase your energy.
- Put an end to common aches and pains.
- Increase emotional and physical health.
- Enjoy life more.

Most people know they live stressful lives, yet they are unaware of how to identify stress in themselves. They become accustomed to a level of tension and assume that this is normal. The following are signs of stress. When you learn to observe them in yourself, it will be easier to learn to redirect the negative energy into a more positive constructive activity.

## *Signs of Stress*

### *Hurry-Sickness*

Are you guilty of any of the "habits" on the following list? Each of these actions can cause you stress and discomfort. Often people are guilty of these "hurry-sickness" traits, without really being aware of how they are hurting themselves.

- Trying to do more in less time.
- Chronically looking at your watch.
- Becoming angry when others seem too slow.
- Feeling locked in a struggle with the clock.

Take the hurry-sickness test. Close your eyes and try to determine when one minute is up. Most people with the "hurry sickness" think a minute has passed when only 15-30 seconds have actually gone by.

### *Tension*

- Muscle tightening (slumping posture, restless movement, e.g., frequent shifting position while sitting in a chair).

- Tiredness/fatigue (Not "it feels so good to sit and relax," but "I'm so tired and I can't sleep" or "I'm tired even when I wake up after a night's sleep").
- Irritability (wanting to distance yourself from other people, an increase in frustration, pessimism, impatience or hostility,).
- Mistakes (drop in your performance, careless errors).
- Distractions (difficulty concentrating, mind wandering, forgetfulness).
- Feeling empty or a heightened sense of vulnerability.
- Aggression or hostility (sudden surges of anger, road rage).

Are you convinced yet that relaxation is a necessity for healthy living? Now that you know what you need to do, do you know how to relax? Most Americans settle on the couch for an evening of mindless television and a beer or bowl of chips to unwind from the day's tension. It's one thing to choose a specific TV show to enjoy. It's quite another to fall victim to mindless staring at the TV for hours at a time. Passive inactivity is not relaxation. True relaxation requires active participation.

*Passive inactivity is not relaxation. True relaxation requires active participation.*

Mary only knew how to relieve stress by eating. She also chose food as a means to take a break from her work. She'd sit in front of the computer getting herself all worked up and never even notice the tension in her body. All she knew was that she felt hungry.

I taught her a process of integrating other forms of relaxation into her workday. I instructed her to use one or two techniques two to three times each day. (see appendix for techniques). She was free to eat if she was still hungry, but first she had to spend one to twenty minutes doing one of the relaxation techniques. At first she insisted she didn't have time to relax, and certainly not two to three times during her work day. I suggested she try it for one week. If she didn't end up having more time to do her work, she could give up my way and go back to her own way.

> ***"The stress actually generates hunger. I was shocked how I was much less interested in food when I took time to relax.."***

After several days integrating these techniques, she was pleasantly surprised on several accounts. For one thing, she had more time to do her work. Because she worked more efficiently, the work went more smoothly. In addition, she found she was far less hungry. "The stress actually generated hunger," said Mary. "I was shocked how I was much less interested in food when I took time to relax."

Make a list of ten things that are relaxing to you. These should include things that will take as little as one minute to twenty minutes and up to several hours. Have the list available, and integrate these into your daily life. Use one of these techniques instead of unhealthy destructive habits from the past. After a while, it will become quite natural to reach for something relaxing instead of chips and the TV. Here are some of the techniques my clients use to relax:

- Computer game
- Walk around the block*
- Ride a bicycle*
- Swim*
- Doodle drawing
- Yoga deep breathing
- Self-hypnosis
- Paint by number
- Bowling
- Horseback riding
- Flip through magazine
- Talk to a friend
- Play with your pet
- Go to a movie
- Drive in the car
- Listen to music
- Meditation
- Put a model together
- Archery
- Stretch
- Plan a vacation (peruse travel brochures)

The suggestions marked with a * are not the same as exercise. They are for pleasure only. A gentle stroll, a pleasure bike ride through the park, or an enjoyable swim are to be done without any fitness goal in mind. Do not put exercise as one of the relaxation choices. Although disciplined physical training usually results in decreased stress, for most people it is just another one of those things they are obligated to do. The purpose of relaxation is to get away from all the "have to's" and get in touch with what you truly want to do at that moment.

### *Candy for Your Body*

Following are some additional techniques for relaxation. Remember, it's important to create a new lifestyle. The only way to create long-term change is to gradually integrate these things into your life. You may find yourself going back to old ways at times. Perhaps you reach for food to relax or to escape from a problem. Don't harp on it. Focus on your success. All you need is one success to use as a reference point. Once you have an experience of how good it feels to use active relaxation instead of passive or destructive types, you will be more apt to bring that to mind when you have an opportunity to make a choice next time. Human beings are naturally drawn to pleasure. When you learn to identify true relaxation as a pleasure state, it will be easy to choose it. Old patterns will fall by the wayside.

Lynne was so thrilled with how relaxation gave her pleasure sensations, she called it, "candy for the body." The relaxation techniques listed in the Appendix (pages 181–191) will give you more suggestions for how to fire food and hire peace to do the job right.

### *Hypnosis or Meditation*

Hypnosis and meditation are forms of deep relaxation. Both rejuvenate your mind and body. Some studies suggest that in hypnosis and meditation, you go into a deeper state of rest than in actual sleep. Learn self-hypnosis or meditation, and you can take this mini-vacation with you wherever you go.

During hypnosis there are measurable changes in brain wave patterns. Beta is the normal state of consciousness, whereas Alpha is the state of hypnosis, where the brain waves have slowed considerably. An even slower wave is called theta (where the heart also slows down). Delta is actual sleep.

While those states occur physiologically, shifts in mental state also take place. In a trance, a person can by-pass the "critical factor," which is the ability to make judgments. Therefore, in hypnosis, personal judgment is temporarily held in abeyance although the person in this state may be totally aware of what is being said. A prominent hypnotist, Hildegard, refers to this awareness as the "hidden observer."

For example, under hypnosis you might receive this suggestion: "Your eyes are shut tight and you can't or won't open them. It's as if they are glued together." Because of your receptive nature in a trance, you want to believe this. The part of your mind that controls the opening and closing of your eyes cooperates with the suggestion. The result: Your eyes respond as if glue is holding them together. At the same time, the "hidden observer" might notice what is happening. You might find yourself saying to yourself, "Wow, I can't believe I can't open my eyes."

Is this blind obedience? Is there danger in it? While individual judgment may be temporarily suspended, it is not banished from existence. Imagine, for example, the part of you that knows how to drive a car. While you are engaged in some other activity, such as reading or watching TV, is the part of you that knows how to drive erased? Of course not. When you need to call upon your driving capabilities, they automatically come forth. By the same token, if there were danger such as a fire or some other need for judgment, a natural survival mechanism would bring the person out of hypnosis fully capable of responding.

### *How Will I Know if I Am in Hypnosis*

Hypnosis is a naturally occurring state. Daydreaming is one instance where it happens in day-to-day life. Perhaps you've driven in a car while preoccupied with one thing or another, and after a few minutes you suddenly look up and feel surprised about how far you've driven. You can't recall the last several miles at all. You were in a state of "highway hypnosis" which is commonly referred to as daydreaming. On one hand, you must have been aware of things going on around you, or you wouldn't have been able to drive without crashing. However, you were so absorbed in your thoughts that you were unaware of your surroundings.

The state of the most profound hypnosis is when you are drifting off to sleep but not in the delta state yet. Perhaps you can recall being in this twilight state when the telephone rang or someone called to you. You may have been vaguely aware of the disruption in the background but were still half asleep. This is what you can expect to experience in hypnosis.

Hypnosis doesn't have any particular feeling to it. It is simply a state of deep relaxation. Some people feel profoundly relaxed. They may feel in a deep day-dreamy state and lose awareness of their environment to some degree. Some people feel that their limbs are very heavy or very light. Others visualize more vividly than normal. Others may feel a little relaxed but not be convinced they are hypnotized.

The key is to realize relaxation, whether mild or profound. Because the experience is varied, do not rely on your subjective perception to determine you are in hypnosis. You will notice some changes in the way you react to stress. At first, you will maintain a degree of relaxation for a short period of time after hypnosis (perhaps an hour or so). You will maintain the state of ease longer throughout the day when you continue to practice hypnosis on a regular basis.

A common question often arises about the difference between meditation and self-hypnosis. The only actual difference is the outcome you wish to achieve. Both processes slow down your brain waves. Meditation is usually used for the purpose of relaxation. Hypnosis also offers the opportunity to rejuvenate your body. However, in hypnosis, you usually intend to condition yourself for a particular result. Perhaps you want to find a solution to a problem or motivate yourself to achieve a goal. The self-hypnosis technique on page 186 will give you a good start.

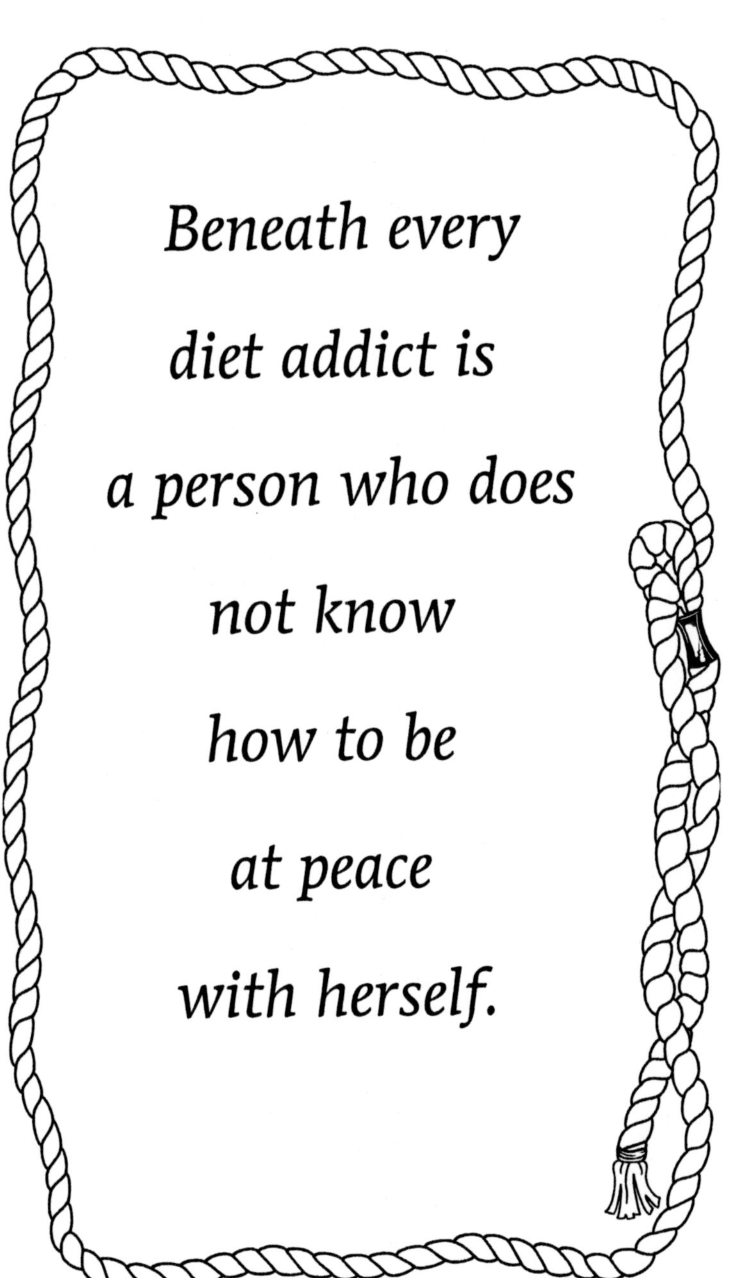

*Beneath every*

*diet addict is*

*a person who does*

*not know*

*how to be*

*at peace*

*with herself.*

## Epilogue:

# The Pursuit of Happiness

*The purpose of life is a life of purpose. This is the true joy in life: To be used for a purpose recognized by yourself as a mighty one.*
George Bernard Shaw, British author

A folktale tells of a traveler going from one village to another. On his journey he comes upon a family going to the village he'd just left. They ask him how nice that village was. "Is it a good place to live? Do people get along? Can a family make a decent living?"

He replies by first asking how they like the village from which they'd just come. They say they like it and were satisfied. "Then you'll like the village you are headed to," he says.

The family thanks him and go on their way. Later, he comes upon another family. Once again, he is asked about the village from which he's just come and again he replies by asking how they felt about their previous home.

This family says, "It was terrible. People fought with each other, had no way to make a decent living, and we were quite unhappy."

"Oh," says the traveler. "I assure you, you will find discontent in the new village as well."

The pursuit of happiness is perhaps the strongest motivation for the never-ending chase for the illusive slim body. We may know happiness can only come from within, but it doesn't stop us from hoping external rewards will bring us the joy we seek. We believe if only we had the house we've dreamed of or the husband we want or financial success, we'd finally be happy.

With the intensity of the junkie's search for his next fix or the alcoholic's quest for one more drink, we get off the couch once again, hit the gym and start the newest diet. The beginning feels great, like the first drink after a period of abstinence. It gives us the high we are looking for. We might think the good feeling comes from finally getting back on track and getting our bodies back in shape. The burst of energy from the exercise certainly helps.

But then the mundane sets in—the ordinary feelings of day-to-day life on a diet and dragging yourself to the gym. Like the alcoholic's satisfaction from the first drink, that now isn't enough; we no longer feel the intensity of the high we had when we first started the diet. We need more.

We are addicted to diets and the pursuit of thinness. This is the major reason for hundreds of new diets each year. With determined resolution that this will be the final answer to our weight problem and unhappiness, we use the next diet like the addict's fix.

Beneath every diet addict is a person who does not know how to be at peace with herself. The same restlessness that stirs the drive for another drink also drives the need for another diet. She hopes this will be the one to fill whatever she is lacking. The only difference between the alcoholic and the dieter is society's attitude. We all agree that an alcoholic should stop drinking. Yet the dieter is encouraged to get on yet another diet. Whether the reason given is for health or appearance, the result is the same: An endless futile quest for happiness through false means. Like the alcoholic who must first stop drinking before he can go to the source of the discontent, the dieter must stop dieting.

If you are unhappy with who you are, having a slim body is just like seeking contentment in another village. You bring yourself with you wherever you go. It is easy to know this intellectually and yet another to know this in your heart. Certainly try to give your body the chance to be at its best. Eat reasonably well, exercise moderately. But realize the limitation of what this will give you. It will be a body at its best; nothing more and nothing less. It doesn't give you happiness.

Having a slimmer body doesn't mean anything. It is only a slimmer body. You may have the ability to move better or fit into smaller clothes. Perhaps that will enable you to like this aspect of yourself better. However, it is limited to just that; you'll move better and fit into slimmer clothes.

Also, realize the limitation of what is your best. You may have an idealized image that you continue to fail to attain. Perhaps you have been unsuccessful because you

> *"I thought that success would bring contentment. But, I found that contentment is a separate process."*
>
> *-Marian*

have unrealistic expectations and not because you are a failure or because you didn't try hard enough.

Many people imagine how dramatically different their lives will be when they get that perfectly acceptable body. Often, they are unrealistic in their expectations. It's similar to people who win millions of dollars with the lottery. Most of them are broke within a few years. This is because they are who they are. Their self-image is of one who doesn't have money.

Marie weighed over 300 pounds. She talked about how she imagined herself when she lost weight. She said she could see herself jump up and suspend in mid-air for a few minutes. She was not talking symbolically about jumping to express her exuberance. She literally meant this. I told her that even a 100-pound person couldn't do this. The law of gravity would bring her back to the ground in a matter of seconds. Her desire to be slim was so desperate, it hadn't occurred to her she'd been grossly distorting what being slim could do for her.

## *The Pursuit of Health*

Do you expect more health from your body than is rightfully yours? Is your pressure to take better care of yourself beyond a reasonable expectation? If you berate yourself for not exercising more or eating better, you probably fall into the "greed is good syndrome."

Some people strive for more health in the same way they pursue a bigger and better car. You can only have so much health. And sometimes, you can't even have as much as you think you ought to have. One client stated that if she didn't want to die, she'd better stick to her rigid diet plan. While she did have some physical problems, flexibility in her eating and exercise program would not sentence her to death.

Americans falsely believe they have control in areas they just don't. The American dream (or should I say, American lie) is that if you work hard enough, you can have anything. If your leg were cut off, would you grow a new one by working hard?

People pressure themselves to work harder in order to have more. It's as if they can't tolerate being told "no." They take on responsibilities that aren't theirs and fail to accept life's limitations.

When is good, enough? When is your best acceptable? This is your health. This is the best you can do at this time with what you've been given. Accept this and get on with using your health for what is intended. Experience the joys of life and let happiness motivate you.

Think of the unhappy family's hunt. The new village was just another place to bring their discontent. Remember the satisfied family's search for a new place to live. Perhaps because of an interest in just experiencing more of life, do the best for yourself and your body. Eat well. Exercise moderately. Appreciate whatever body God has given you. Then get on with the joy of living.

## *Enjoy Life More*

The ultimate stress reliever: The simplicity of enjoying life as it is. This is undoubtedly the best thing you can do for yourself. Ask yourself, at life's end, how do you want to be remembered? What do you want to be able to say about your own life? Get in the habit of monthly or weekly reflections. Vividly imagine what others would say about you in a eulogy. Are you living that life? If not, what can you do to devote yourself to that life?

*Your understanding of the concepts presented in this book will be greatly enhanced by practicing and repeating these exercises on a regular basis.*

# Appendix

***Exercises***

You are not your mind. Therefore, you have the power to control the thinking that goes on in your mind. This thinking affects your behavior and your feelings about yourself. Imagine what it would be like to create only thoughts that encourage a sense of well-being and security!

You can. Here is an exercise to teach you how. First, experience the "cause and effect" connection between your mind and your experience of yourself.

1. Close your eyes and take a nice deep relaxing breath.
2. Picture a mountain lake and notice the gentle movement of the water, back and forth.
3. Now imagine your mind is the water and its rhythm. Do this until you feel somewhat relaxed and able to tap into your imagination freely.
4. Now imagine a big juicy lemon. Picture the yellow color and the texture and anything else that makes it seem as vivid and real as possible. If you

have trouble visualizing, just think about the lemon, its color and texture, etc. The thought process, even without a mental picture, will also bring about the physiological response.

5. Now imagine taking a big bite of the lemon and the sour juice filling your mouth.

6. Notice how your mouth responds. Do your cheeks and lips pucker as if you really had the lemon in your mouth? Can you see how your mental imagery created this response? The lemon wasn't actually there, yet your body responded as if it were.

Did you experience the connection between the mental thoughts/pictures and the response in your body? Now you are ready to change your thinking.

Your understanding of the concepts presented in this book will be greatly enhanced by practicing and repeating these exercises on a regular basis. The exercises that follow will give you that "hands-on" experience. They are listed in a specific suggested order; however, feel free to go back and repeat any previous activity whenever you feel it will help you.

### *Self-Esteem Exercises*

If you've spent your life trying to fix your body and your food obsession, it's time to put those things aside and find some new interests in life.

Here are exercises that will help you to create a focus for your life. For each step, write down everything that comes to mind in response to the following questions. When you think you have nothing left to express, continue to write anything. The idea is to keep the pen moving. Usually some emotional blocks get in the way. In order to get past these resistances, it is crucial to continue writing. You may repeat a few sentences you've already written. This will help you keep the process going. Your mind will go on a search for more information because you are giving it the message that you are not finished. Your "other than conscious mind" will continue to bring forth ideas.

*Life Values Part One*

Can you set aside time each day to make sure you are spending your time in ways that are meaningful to you? Catch yourself thinking of things that don't support your emotional well-being. When you have negative body-size thoughts, stop! Ask yourself what thoughts would better serve you. Then redirect your focus of attention.

1. What am I doing now with my life? What have I been putting off (writing, going to school, traveling, changing jobs)? What do I want to accomplish?
2. Imagine you know you have only five years to live. What would you do with your time? What would be important to accomplish?
3. Now imagine you have only six months to live. Would you do anything else differently?

4. Now imagine you have only one month to live. Get very specific about how you would spend your day-to-day life. Chances are you wouldn't be thinking about how many calories your meal has. You'd eat it and enjoy every minute of it. Thoughts of body size would also become irrelevant. You'd more likely think of how this body is here to help you experience life and the joys of living. You might want to take the time to think about what contribution you made to the world around you. Did you treat the people in your life in the best way you could?
5. Now imagine you have only one day to live. Simply breathing the fresh air would more than likely be a joyful experience. How would you spend your time? With whom?
6. What did you learn from this exercise? Did you realize some of your true values?
7. Now realize that you have a lifetime to live. Live it with the same degree of appreciation as if you only had one month or a week. How can you spend more time thinking and doing things that reflect who you really are?

*Life Values Part Two*

In order to put body-image in perspective, we have to bring out all that is important about you.

1. In order to do this, imagine you live in a world that is blind. Your body is not only, not of para-

mount importance, but it is not visually noticed... ever. How your body looks is irrelevant to your life's enjoyment. Now imagine your mind is free to focus on everything else about yourself. Your obsession about your body is gone.

2. Ask yourself what is important to you now. What would you like to spend your time thinking about? What would you like to spend your time doing?

3. Take out a piece of paper and imagine going through an average day. Start with what you normally do each day. Do you look in the mirror and criticize what you see before you get in the shower? If you and the rest of the world were blind, what would be different about this? What would you think about before you get in the shower? Then consider the next thing that you normally do. Do you put your clothes on and again judge yourself for your protruding stomach or thunder thighs? Now imagine what you would think about while you got dressed if you couldn't see yourself. You would probably shift your awareness from what your body looks like, to how your body feels.

Remember, once you do this exercise, you will put your body image back into your daily experience, but in a more appropriate proportion to the rest of your life.

### *Stop "Shoulding" on Yourself*

One way to test if you are living your life values or someone else's is to see if you are shoulding on yourself. Choose two of the following four sentences for each experiment.

- I want
- I don't want
- I choose
- I choose not

Catch yourself saying "I should" or "I shouldn't." For example: "I should clean my house." Choose two of the above sentences that apply. For example:

- I don't want to clean my house and I choose to do it anyway.
- I don't want to clean my house and I choose not to do it right now.

Brainstorm for options. Perhaps you could choose how clean it really has to be. You could simply make it livable and not insist it meet unnecessary expectations. Maybe you could hire a housecleaning service. Now you are free to enjoy the time on the things you value most. Be careful about saying you don't have the money. Once again, it is a matter of values. You allocate money in ways that reflect your values. Even if money is tight, review these choices too. Is it possible, at times, you automatically pull the wallet out without making a conscious choice? Or perhaps you're saving your money for your retirement or children's college funds. Here again, you are making life value choices. If putting that few dollars a month into your retirement is more important than hiring someone to clean your house, then accept that as your life value. Choose it and enjoy living with it.

### *Body Image Exercises*

Are you convinced yet that your negative attitude is not solely of your own making? Society has played its part by promoting ideas through the media. Are you ready to take charge of your life and create a positive body-image? Are you ready to reject those influences that reinforce your negativity? Take the challenge!

Many times, our reflective assumptions from the past go unchallenged in our minds. As stated in the Body Image chapter, it is important to bring forth memories from the past that influenced your current attitudes about your body. Following is a sample of my own reflective associations from my past:

> "The ugliest part of a woman is the back of her knees." (I heard someone say this when I was 15 years old. I remember feeling such disgust at her negativity.)
>
> My mother used to tell me I have eyes like Elizabeth Taylor. (I remember feeling so proud of this.)

> "Your body is more from your father's side of the family. You're built more like your father's mother."

> I remember my mother comparing my shoulders to hers and pointing out how much more broad mine were than hers or those of my sisters.

> My aunt remarked, with surprise, at how broad the palm of my hand is.

> After I leaped to hit a tennis ball with my racket, my aunt remarked, "Look how graceful she is."

This is a small sample of the things I remember being said during my childhood. Once you remember these things, how your body image was formed will become clear. For example, I always felt I had a strong body. I was told that my father's mother was a strong woman and that my body was from her side of the family. (She lived healthy and in her own apartment by herself until she died at 95.) Now I can trace this belief to the source.

This is not a problem when you are told positive things about yourself. However, when you bring forth the negative things you were told when you were growing and formulating your body image, you will be able to challenge the truth and validity of those things and transcend their negative hold on you.

Here's an example: I remember being told that I was born fat. I accepted it as the way it has always been for me. Then one day I looked at some old pictures of myself as a child. These photos showed someone different than the image I had always internalized from what my mother had always said about me. I certainly wasn't skinny. But I wasn't fat either. I had a bit of a stomach, and I was chubby. But judging from the pictures, I certainly wasn't as huge as I was told or led to believe. Once I discovered this, I was able to reach within and make a shift in the way I perceived myself.

This is not about blaming your past. It is more about taking responsibility for the ideas you have been holding on to and making a choice about them now.

The following exercise will help you bring forth those ideas from the past that have shaped your thinking.

*Reflection & Association Exercise*

1. Reflect on everything and anything that you've heard or read about your body during the time you were growing up. These ideas and images are how you formulate your beliefs about yourself.
2. Write everything on paper. Don't censor. Perhaps you can recall a cliché when you were ten. Maybe you remember something your father said about how you have your mother's smile.
3 .Keep the pen moving even if you run out of things to write. You can re-write something you've written previously. By the time you get half through with that repeated thought, a new one will likely come to mind. Push past moments when nothing comes to mind.

4. Do this several times. Drawing a blank is just part of the process of getting to the deeper memories. After a short time of thinking of nothing new, more thoughts will come to you.
5. Look at each comment that has surfaced. Ask yourself how each comment makes you feel. Enjoy the positive ones.
6. Challenge the negative ones by either:
Finding a new point of view (e.g., instead of "Women are more attractive when they are small and dainty," try "Large women are soft and cuddly and wonderful to hold."),

*or*

Repeating the negative phrase over and over and over again, then repeating its opposite. (For example, "I should be small and dainty to be attractive." Say this five to ten times out loud. Then repeat five to ten times, "I am attractive with my round and soft body.")

Continue alternating the two until you notice a shift in your feelings on the subject. You will have a sense of relief from the negative and a new place in your mind for the positive.

*How to Change Negative Thinking*

1.Periodically and randomly, several times each day, stop and notice what you are thinking.

2. If it is a neutral or positive thought,

- Acknowledge the thought;
- Observe how you've been feeling; and
- Make the connection between the thought and the feeling. You may recognize the "cause and effect" immediately, or it may take several times before you do. Be patient. The connection will come.

3. If it is a negative thought,

- Acknowledge the thought;
- Observe how it contributes to the feeling you have (e.g., your chest is tight, you feel like screaming, etc.);
- Recognize the cause and effect between your thoughts and feelings; and
- Ask yourself what other point of view you could have about it. Don't force the different point of view on yourself; just ask what other point of view you could have.

For example, let's say you thought, "Why am I so weak that I can't stick to a diet?" There are many other interpretations of this same thing, such as:

- "I enjoy food and the freedom to choose different foods."
- "I prefer eating what I like and weighing more, rather than feeling restricted."

- "My food temptation is understandable. I've had this impulsive nature all my life. I have made many successful changes with it and am continuing to work at it at a pace that is right for me.

Imagine how much better you'd feel about yourself with one of the more positive interpretations!

Nothing is intrinsically good or bad about anything. The meaning we bring to it determines its value. Consider the following story, which will help you understand this point.

There's a cliché about a glass being half empty or half full. However, another viewpoint would say that it simply is what it is... half a glass of liquid. But suppose you were thirsty and all you had to drink was this half glass of water, which didn't satisfy your thirst. You'd more than likely see it as half empty. If you really got dramatic (as most of us do), you might carry on about how you asked your daughter to leave the glass full because the repair crew would be turning off the water for a few hours... and now you're left with your thirst and no way to quench it... unless you get in your car and drive to the store to buy some... and you can't find your car keys. Why doesn't your daughter ever listen to you anyway? You surely would make yourself (and your daughter) miserable with this kind of thinking, wouldn't you?

Now suppose the same half glass of water did satisfy your thirst. Wasn't your daughter such an angel to remember to leave you some water? Your daughter's reality may have had nothing to do with thoughts of you. Perhaps on her way out the door, she got thirsty, filled a glass of water, and drank only half. Because she was in a hurry, she left the rest on the counter. She didn't give a thought one way or the other about you or the repair crew.

Each of these views are potential meanings you could attach to half a glass of water. The glass has no meaning in and of itself; it is just a half glass of water. Your decision to see it as half empty or half full creates meaning for you. And this meaning is what you brought to it.

What if instead you call it what it is, without meaning? I'm thirsty; I drank this half glass of water, and I'm still thirsty. Therefore, I need to find more water. Notice how the emotions are gone. The situation is what it is, and there is no need for anger or upset.

In my life, I prefer to take a more neutral or positive point of view unless my perspective is shown to be wrong. It saves me aggravation and generally allows me to go through life feeling reasonably good. It has taken practice to get here, but I am at the point now that this thinking is quite automatic.

Practice this by catching yourself in thought. Whatever your thought may have been, find two or three different perspectives you could take as well.

### *Body Image Focus Shift Exercise*

1. Close your eyes and picture yourself on a movie screen.
2. Notice the different aspects of the picture, such as: Is the picture color or black and white? From what distance are you viewing the picture? Are you looking at the total you, or zeroing in on a particular part?

3. Now imagine someone looking at you who finds you attractive. Notice the same elements as before. What is the difference? Is that person looking at your total body? Does that person see you from a further distance?
4. Change your perspective and view it from the same one as the person who finds you attractive.

*Talking Parts*

People who have a strong ability for "self-talk" will find this exercise easy enough to do. Those who do not, can adapt it. For example, you may draw a picture, or imagine a picture representation in your mind. To convert the exercise into a visual mode, you could see yourself clutching your stomach at the thought of putting pizza in it. Maybe you'd then see a big loud mouth shouting at you, "I want pizza."

When you find you are reaching out for food, first stop and ask yourself the following questions. They will help you make good food choices for good reasons.

1. Am I hungry? If so, what part of me is hungry? Is it my mouth, my stomach, my mind, my face? (Yes, your face can be hungry. One day when my face was hungry, I rubbed food all over it. I was quite surprised at how wonderfully satisfying it was, and it completely relieved my need to eat the food.)
2. If your stomach is hungry, fine. Ask it what it's hungry for.

3. If your stomach wants one thing and another part of you wants another, have them negotiate. For example: Let's imagine your head wants pizza. It's been thinking of pizza for the last few days, and you haven't had an opportunity to get any. Ask your stomach if this is what it wants too. If it says yes, go ahead and have some and enjoy it.
4. If your stomach says no, ask it what it does want. Suppose your stomach remembers that the last time it ate pizza, it didn't digest well, leaving it feeling upset and uncomfortable. Have your stomach tell this to your head, and ask your head if it would be willing to choose something that is more agreeable. If it says yes, great. Choose something else.
5. However, your mind may be stubborn and insist that pizza is what it wants. Let the conversation continue until there is some sort of resolution. For example:

Head: I want pizza. I don't care that it upsets you.

Stomach: Okay, I can hear that you really want pizza. If I agree to it, would you be willing to eat slowly so I can digest it better? And would you be willing to pay attention to when I've had enough and not force more into me? When you continue eating after I've had enough, I usually ache.

Head: Yes, I would be willing to listen to your needs.

6. The idea is to get agreement between the two parts. One part should not bully the other. If it does, continue the conversation until there is some degree of cooperation.
7. If a part other than your stomach is hungry, ask it what it wants. Ask it if it could have anything in the world that it really wants, what would it be? Is there something other than food that would satisfy it? For example, "My abdomen feels tense and wants some relief."

Offer it suggestions, other than food, that will give it what it needs. Perhaps you could place your palms flat on the surface of your abdomen and feel the warmth from your hands soothing you. Then ask your abdomen if this is satisfying its need. If it is, great. If not, try something else. Perhaps it needs a real good belly laugh. Find a funny book or movie to stimulate laughter. Check in again with your abdomen. Has this created some relief? Keep trying different things until you satisfy the true need.

*My Features Exercise*

Write down all your attractive features. If you're not accustomed to thinking in this positive way, you may need some help jogging your thought process. Here is a list to help you get started:

Smooth skin
Nice hair color
Nice color eyes
Long legs
Pretty eyes
Shapely buttocks
Pleasant smile
Sensuous lips

Nicely shaped eye brows | Shapely legs
Regardless of size, perhaps you are in good proportion

The selective attention toward your negative features can now be replaced with awareness of these positive ones.

- Catch yourself when you have a negative body thought, and replace it with one of your new-found positive ones.
- Realize that your black-and-white thinking ("Beauty or Beast") is no longer necessary, i.e., you may be larger than the average woman, but perhaps you do have good proportions or shapely legs.

*Food Exercises*

The purpose of these exercises is to help you get in touch with the food you truly want at the time you want it. With this awareness, you will no longer grab for food for fear it will be taken away from you with the next diet. You will have confidence in choosing food at the time you want it, feel the satisfaction, and learn to save the rest for a later time when you are hungry and more likely to want it. Therefore, you won't have to force it on yourself when you have had enough to eat.

### *Planned Binge or Paradox*

If you are one to restrict your food and then binge, do the food meditation exercise along with a planned binge. A planned binge is when you deliberately and consciously plan a time for a binge. In advance of the time for your planned binge, go to the store and buy twice the amount of food you think you can eat at one sitting. Set all of it out in front of you. Then do the Food Meditation process. If bingeing is not the issue for you, do the food meditation on its own at your next meal or snack. The purpose of the planned binge is to help you find your true level of satisfaction.

When you are free to relax and eat what you truly want, without judgment and restriction, you will discover that you don't want to eat the amount you thought you did. Another name for this is "the paradox." When you allow yourself to eat, the opposite happens. When you give yourself permission to eat without fear, the paradox is guaranteed.

### *Food Meditation*

Decide on a time when you can be alone in your own home. Buy the foods you like, and spread them out in front of you. Take a moment to look at all the food. Tell yourself you can eat as much as you want and whatever type you want, as long as you are "awake and conscious when you eat."

Now look at the food. Notice the color and the texture. Scan the array of foods. Notice which food appeals to you at this particular moment. Reach for it and bring it closer to your mouth-but before you put it into your mouth, smell it. Ask yourself if it smells as you thought it would? Disconnect from the memory of your past experience of this food. Stay in the moment with it. Now look at it again. Does it look different than when it was further away and on the table? Now put it into your mouth. Notice the flavor. Does it taste as you thought it would? Is the taste different than the smell would have you believe it would taste?

Notice the texture. Is it smooth, hard, crunchy? Does it make a sound when you chew it? What is the temperature? Is it warm, hot, cold? Pay attention and savor the flavor.

You will find that you will be able to do this for a while. Then, more than likely, you will find you go unconscious. (I know a further explanation of going unconscious is not necessary. Just giving it a name will make you aware of the very thing you have been doing all along.) The moment you realize that you've gone unconscious, stop what you are doing, put the food down, take a deep breath and begin the process of looking, smelling, etc. again.

### *Step-by-Step Food Meditation*

It is crucial to let down your defenses when you do this technique. Guilt about eating drives the need to go unconscious when you eat because it feels like a shameful thing to do. To help you prepare enough of the right type of foods, ask yourself what foods you would choose if you didn't have health concerns or worries about weight gain (for example, sweets, fried foods, fast food, etc.). This will help you choose freely without regard to consequences. Only then will you be able to pay true attention to your experience of the food.

1. Choose an atmosphere of safety where you will not be judged, preferably when you are alone and can let down your guard.
2. Play baroque music in the background (this will slow your heartbeat down to 60 beats per minute and slow your brain waves down too). It will enable you to stay in touch with your experience of your body.
3. Set out enough of a variety of food. This will enable you to truly discover what foods you like and don't like, instead of reacting from memory about the last time you ate them.
4. Take all the foods you have bought and spread them out in front of you. Take a moment to look at all the food. Tell yourself you can eat as much as you want and whatever type you want, as long as you are "awake and conscious when you eat."
5. Now look at the food. Notice the color and the texture. Scan the array of foods. Notice which food appeals to you at this particular moment. Reach for it and bring it closer to your mouth, but before you put it into your mouth, smell it. Ask yourself whether or not it smells the way you thought it would.
6. Disconnect from the memory of your past experience of this food. Stay in the moment with it.

Now look at it again. Does it look different than when it was further away and on the table?

7. Now put it into your mouth. Notice the flavor. Does it taste as you thought it would? Is the taste different than the smell would have you believe?

8. Notice the texture. Is it smooth, hard, crunchy? Does it make a sound when you chew it? What is its temperature? Is it warm, hot, cold? Pay attention and savor the flavor.

Have you noticed how perfume held continuously under your nose will seem to lose its scent? There is a similar reaction with food. Stop and pay attention to your experience of the taste of the food. Notice that when you are quite hungry, food is tasty. With each bite, your body gets more satisfied. Notice how the food feels when it reaches your stomach, and continue to notice everything about the eating experience. Notice that when you have had enough nutrition, the food does not taste as good. Notice the difference in taste between when you started eating and when you are satisfied. In addition to the feeling of satisfaction in your stomach, the change in taste will make you want to stop eating. Now you are responding to your body.

9. You will find that you will be able to do this for a while. Then, more than likely you will find you go unconscious. (I know a further explanation of "going unconscious" is not necessary. Just giving it

a name will make you aware of the very thing you have been doing all along.)

10. The moment you realize that you've gone unconscious, stop what you are doing. Put the food down, take a deep breath, and begin the process of looking, smelling, etc.

11. Remind yourself you can eat as much as you want, whatever type of food you want, at any time that you want, as long as you are "awake and conscious when you eat."

*Body Talk: Discover Your True Need*

- Notice if you are at peace with a food choice. If your thought is that you "shouldn't" eat this, then you are in conflict.
- If you are at odds about it, stop, close your eyes and get in touch with what part of you is unhappy with the choice.
- Negotiate with the different parts.
- Find out the true need and decide what will atisfy this.
- •Consider these as possible true needs:
  - Tired
  - Need comfort
  - Need release of anger, sadness, or another emotion

For example, let's say you had a knee-jerk reaction for eating, but you stopped yourself before putting food in your mouth, and asked yourself if you were hungry. You check in with your stomach, and it was nutritionally satisfied. You checked in with your mouth, and it didn't really have a particular need for food. You asked what part of you wanted to eat. It turns out your mind told you it wanted to eat. You could have a conversation like this:

Self: You say you want food, but do you realize your stomach and mouth don't.

Mind: Yes.

Self: What is the true need you have now? What are you trying to fulfill with food?

Mind: I don't really know, except that I'm aware of feeling overwhelmed by all that I have to do and the deadline I have to meet.

Self: It sounds like you'd like a solution to the problem.

Mind: Well, I suppose. But what I really want is to get away from it all.

Self: Ah! So it sounds like your true need is to escape.

Mind: Yes, but I know I shouldn't do that.

Self: Why not?

Mind: I don't know. It just seems wrong.

Self: What's wrong is to use food as an escape. But there are many healthy escapes that will leave you refreshed and better able to cope with your problems.

Mind: Like what?

Self: If you could have anything you truly want, what would it be?

Mind: I'd like it if my mind could quiet down and stop this chatter.

Self: What would help it do that?
Mind: A funny movie.
Self: Great. Why don't you take a couple of hours and escape to a movie?
Mind: It's really okay to give myself what I need?
Self: You bet. By the way, how's the need to eat?
Mind: It's gone.

*Integrate a Healthy Lifestyle*

This exercise shows you how to slowly integrate good healthy eating into your lifestyle, without causing a backlash of rebellion and cravings for negative eating choices.

First select foods you know to be good for you. Isolate a day in which you eat only those foods. Notice how you feel. Does the food sustain you longer before hunger strikes? Keep that stored in your memory. Do the same thing when eating foods that are not high in nutrient content. What does it feel like? Do you find yourself compulsive or needing to satisfy more urges? Do you have more disruptive food thoughts throughout the day? Notice this without any judgment about it. Now store this in your memory bank.

The next time you reach for food, ask yourself what experience you would like for that day. Recall what foods gave you which experience. Make your choice for that meal or that day only. The reason to keep the focus on the immediate time is to prevent the various psychological traps that perpetuate the "all-or-nothing syndrome."

If you choose to eat a substantial meal full of nutrition, you are not trapped into living this way forever. Unlike a diet, you are not locked into it or need to feel guilty for going off. You can certainly feel free to make a choice for a "less than nutritious food" at another time if you wish to. (Notice I did not refer to foods as good or bad, right or wrong or cheating or not cheating. These value judgments keep you in a cycle of feeling bad, feeling stressed about feeling bad, and then needing food to compensate for these feelings.) If you choose the less-than-nutritious food, it too is a choice for that moment. It breaks the perpetual, "Oh well, I blew it. I might as well eat anything and everything."

### *Making Behavior Changes*

People whose eating pattern is to skip breakfast and perhaps eat something for lunch but not anything substantial will find themselves eating non-stop throughout the evening. Nutritionally, they have allowed the body to get too hungry. Then nothing will satisfy.

If this is your pattern, perhaps you want to experiment with eating breakfast. On the days that you make this change, notice if your urge to eat through the evening lessens (people who crave sweets may find that eating protein for breakfast will substantially reduce the need for sweets later in the day). Personalize your experimentation. Write a list of food behaviors you want to change. Here are some ideas:

- Eliminate eating on the run.
- Eliminate eating in the car.
- Eliminate taking a second portion.

- Eat breakfast.
- Learning to eat a meal, and then immediately refocus on the next task, instead of lingering with food.

Write a list of food choices you might want to work on. Here are some ideas:

- Eliminate or reduce sweets.
- Eliminate or reduce fried food.
- Eliminate or reduce fast foods.
- Increase water consumption.
- Reduce soda consumption.
- Increase cooking in no-fat liquids such as water or broth.
- Exchange refined carbohydrates for whole grains.

Remember take one or two at a time. Make a solid change in that area before you go on to the next. This entire process will never end because there is always more to do. However, you will find long periods, perhaps years, in which you are satisfied with your eating and behavior patterns.

*To order your self-hypnosis tape, use order form in back of book*

***Imagery Exercises***

*Your Natural Size*

After the above changes, you are finally ready to find your natural size. However, don't attempt this until you have changed some of your attitudes and behaviors from previous exercises, otherwise, you will fall into a diet mentality.

1 .Sit back, close your eyes, take a nice deep breath and relax. Ask yourself the question, if you were just one percent closer to the body size that is healthy for you physically, mentally, and emotionally, what would that be? You can answer in pounds, inches, or clothing size. For example, "If I were 1% closer, I'd weigh 2 pounds less" or "I'd be 1/2 inch smaller around my stomach, hips, and back" or "I'd be 1/2 of a smaller size."
2. Now imagine a colorful hot air balloon. The balloon is used as a vehicle to communicate from your conscious mind to your unconscious mind (sometimes called your wisdom self or your higher self). Your wisdom self is here to help you achieve your goals. It exists to serve you. But you must ask the question in just the right way. State your question in positive terms, make it specific, and make it measurable. For example, you would never say, "I don't want to weigh this much any more." It is far too vague. Your unconscious mind could guide you to eat more food and add a couple of pounds. You would no longer weigh "this much" anymore, would you? That is not what you want. To formulate the request you might say, "Higher self, please guide me to eat the right foods in the appropriate portions that will support my body at 1% closer to my right size."

3. Now that you have established a concrete physical goal, you will ask your wisdom self to guide you toward it. Put your request in the hot air balloon.
4. Formulate your request in one of two ways. You can:
   - Create a picture that represents what you want.
   - Imagine writing the request perhaps in the sky with smoke or chalk or on a piece of paper.
5. Now with closed eyes, picture and imagine that you put your request in the balloon. (Some people can actually see it; others can only sense the balloon or think of a balloon in their mind's eye. It is not necessary to actually see a picture.)
6. Release the balloon and watch it float up toward the sky. Imagine it lifting past the tallest trees toward the clouds. Now see it go beyond the clouds until you can no longer see it.
7. Open your eyes and go about your day-to-day business. You will discover an automatic response to food which will support your new goal. You may notice you eat smaller amounts or you choose foods with more efficient calories.

You may want to use the hot air balloon technique each night before you go to sleep. (The whole process should take between one to five minutes.) In order to be sure you stay away from preoccupation with food or body thoughts, make sure you only measure your success with the scale or tape measure once per month. The main focus of measuring success should be that which is explained in

Chapter 6. (To order an audio self-hypnosis tape for this technique, see page 199.)

### Fitness Exercises

#### *Eliminate "All-or-Nothing" Destructive Exercise Patterns*

First, set a minimum amount of exercise. If you are now just getting back into the exercise routine after having been away for a while, set a goal which is reachable under any circumstances. If you have to work 20 extra hours that week, and your house flooded and the baby sitter quit, ask yourself how much exercise could you do under these extreme situations.

I tell some clients that five minutes once per week is sufficient. They usually balk at this because they know it is not enough to accomplish any real fitness. I tell them that fitness is not the first goal of exercise. Developing some success and a livable routine that they can maintain over time is the first goal. Of course, those who are accustomed to more of a disciplined pattern may set their minimum goal as once per week for 20 minutes or twice per week for ten minutes each time. Remember, choose a pattern you can do under almost any of life's demands. Once you understand this entire pattern, you can decide the appropriate amount for yourself. However, it is important to understand the entire concept before you create your guidelines.

Next, set a maximum amount of exercise each week. The purpose of this is to prevent burn-out. You want the maximum to be sufficient to get you reasonably healthy. You should determine an amount you can manage under average circumstance of your life. I like to use the President J.F. Kennedy guidelines of 20 to 30 minutes three times per week. New research, however, says that the 30 minutes does not have to be all in a row. It will do as much good for your body if you do three ten-minute sessions in one day.

Many studies show this low level of exercise is enough to affect longevity, general health, and risk of heart disease or stroke. In addition, the benefit of this amount of physical activity reduces insulin levels. Insulin stimulates fat storage. Exercise is one of the few things, unlike diets, associated with changing insulin levels and reducing body fat.

Since 20 minutes, three times per week, is enough to do the job, why then, unless you really enjoy exercise, would you demand that you exercise more? Some may be misinformed about the amount necessary. However, in my practice, I have observed how some use the excessive behavior almost as a punishment for not being good enough. Ask yourself what it's been doing for you. Has it just been a habit pattern? Have you believed this was the only way to be fit? Now that you know excessive exercise is not necessary, will you allow yourself to relax with it?

The third step is to accept the minimum and maximum routines as part of your overall pattern. Some weeks, for whatever reason, you will not do more than your minimum. Because you will feel good about reaching your goal, even at its minimum, you will stay motivated to reach your higher goals.

Life has biorhythms. Some days you have more energy than others. Some weeks life hands you more problems than others. When you allow for these differences by being flexible with your expectations, you will always be successful. When you are successful, you feel good and want to continue. Now isn't this far different than the pattern described earlier which put you at the top for a couple of months and then at the bottom for years?

*Redirect Stress: Five-Minute Techniques*

Five minutes, once or twice a day, will reduce stress, restore energy, and make life more enjoyable. Try some of the following:

*Laughter*

Norman Cousins said, "Laughter is inner jogging." He certainly qualifies as an authority. After his doctors pronounced him terminally ill, he checked out of the hospital and into a hotel room armed with comedy movies and books of every type of humor. He laughed himself well. His doctors had predicted he had only months to live. He lived long enough to write 14 books about the subject.

Take time to write about funny things you've experienced. I have a slew of memories of funny things my kids have said or done. I often call on these to "dig my way out of a dismal ditch." Other times, I read a funny book or tell a joke.

*One-Touch Relaxation*

Touch your jaw joints just in front of your ear. Inhale and clench your jaw for five seconds. Release your jaw by letting the lower jaw drop. Relax your tongue by letting the tip rest on your lower front teeth. Exhale. Focus your attention on the contrast between tension and release. Next, clench your jaw using half the tension, then 1/4, then 1/8 tension.

*Take a Dream Break*

Think of your favorite vacation spot. Close your eyes or stare off into the distance and imagine what it is like being there. Research proves that brain chemicals will release according to things imagined. In fact, the minute muscles move according to what you visualize. If you recall a horror movie, your muscles will tense. If you dream of enjoying a day at the beach, your muscles will relax.

*Sharpening your Senses*

Right now, notice what you've been thinking, the chair you're sitting in, the color of hair of the person in front of you, the lighting in the room, the sounds around you, the feeling of your feet in your shoes, etc. Take a few moments to see, hear, and feel the things in your experience in the moment. This wonderful technique can be done anywhere. Do this when standing on the bank line, riding in the car, or even sitting at the computer.

*Body Scan*

Whether you are sitting or standing, stop what you're doing and take a mental scan of the sensations in your body. Notice all the feelings in the features in your face, your eyes, cheeks, lips, chin, jaw. How do they feel? Any tension? Breathe in and imagine directing that breath to the particular part of your body that feels tense. Then release the breath and imagine all the tension leaving. Now, focus on the next section of your body (your neck and shoulders) and do the same thing. Do this for your entire body.

### *Yoga Alternate-Nostril Breathing*

Increase your energy with this technique. Using your thumb and middle finger, you will alternate closing and opening one nostril at a time. First, close your right nostril and breathe in through your left nostril slowly to the count of four. Then hold your breath for the count of four. Now close the left nostril, open the right one and breathe out for the count of six. Next, breathe into the right nostril, (the one from which you just released the air) to the count of four, hold for four, and release from left to the count of six. The next round, you will increase the count. Into the left (the one you just released) to the count of six, hold breath for six, release air out of right to the count of eight. Do the entire process two or three times.

### *Eye Strain*

Even eye strain is enough to cause tension in the rest of your body. If you've been working close up such as with reading, change your focus. Blink several times in a row, then look at things in the distance such as a tree across the street. If you've been looking at far off things, than switch to close things. Brighten or dim the lighting. Step outside for 60 seconds. Move your seat closer or further from a window.

### *Liming*

Liming is the Caribbean art of "doing nothing, guilt-free." I'll never forget the epitome of this during a vacation in Hawaii. Three construction workers stood at a building sight. While one dug a hole with a jackhammer, two others stood next to him doing nothing in particular. You don't need a certain atmosphere for liming. Forget the easy chair, dim lighting, and soft music. You don't need a beer or anything else. Just hang-out with yourself for a while.

### *Relaxation Response Key*

We all have associations with songs, places we've visited, or certain articles of clothing or mementos. These items bring back memories of an experience from the past. A relaxation response key is anything that triggers a relaxation memory. Find something that serves this purpose. The best thing is something you can carry around with you and use it any time you need it.

You can also create a new one. I give clients a phrase to repeat in their minds. "The sun is warm, the grass is green." This is quite soothing. You can use this phrase in conjunction with a physical conditioned response. Take your index finger and touch it to the thumb of the same hand, forming a circle. Use the circled fingers each time you say the phrase. Since this is a conditioned response, the more you use it, the more effective it is. Try it when you're waiting on the bank line or driving in your car.

### *Increase Intimacy*

Human contact, a positive and supportive social network, helps us resist the tension that contributes to disease. Duke University Medical Center conducted a 9-year study with 1368 patients for cardiac catheterization to diagnose heart disease. Those patients with neither a spouse nor friend were three times more likely to die than those involved in caring relationships. People who named five or more friends and relatives who discussed matters important to them were 60% more likely to feel "very happy" than those who could name no such confidantes.

1. Put your name in the center of a circle you draw on a piece of paper. In the outer circle write the names of the closest friends that are a source of warmth and approval. These should be nurturing people, those you are comfortable with, able to confide in, or share meals with.
2. In the inner circle, list old friends you haven't talked to in a while or new friends you'd like to get to know better.
3. Reflect on the type of support you've received from and given to them. Keep the list in prominent place. Periodically, take time to:

- Write a note
- Buy a gift for one of them

- Cut out an article in a magazine you think would be of interest and send it
- Call them on the telephone
- Have lunch with them

## *Attaining Hypnosis Exercises*

### *Self-Hypnosis Technique*

Begin with a narrowing of your focus of attention. You may use an external focus such as a candle to stare at or a spot on the wall. You can choose an internal focus, such as a repeated mental visualization. A scene of the ocean waves rushing in to shore and then out again is quite effective. Another excellent one is to imagine you are walking down a set of one hundred steps. Virtually any mental image you choose will work, however, the best ones are those that are repetitious.

The mind is like a chained wild horse. It wants to be free to drift in the direction of its choosing at any given moment. Drifting to other thoughts may happen when you practice this technique. While you are staring at the candle or repeating the ocean scene, your mind will think of that paperwork you left undone at the office or the project you have facing you at home. When you notice this, gently bring your mind back to your intended focus of attention. Do this repeatedly whenever other thoughts distract you. It is necessary to observe the intruding thought without judgment about it. It is part of the process. Sometimes you will find that your mind drifts frequently. At other times, you will find a steady concentration for long periods.

Continue the process of focused attention until you feel the relaxation in your muscles or your mind slows down. You may experience periods of time in which you have no conscious thought. This is the ultimate.

If your eyes are open and you are focused on an external item, continue to stare at it until your eyes feel like they want to close. Let them close. Sometimes, for some people, the experience of wanting to close their eyes doesn't seem to happen. Instead, they get a fixed stare and tunnel vision. Tunnel vision is when you see a darkening or graying of the light in the room. A tunnel may appear to form between you and the spot you have your gaze fixed on. This is open eyes hypnosis. Hypnosis is not a state of eyelids; it is a state of mind. Eventually, even with tunnel vision, you will feel compelled to close your eyes. Gently close them and enjoy the relaxation.

### *Deepening Techniques*

To deepen your experience you may open your eyes and re-fix your gaze on the same spot. Do this for several moments and then close your eyes again. Notice how much deeper your relaxation is when you close your eyes the second time. Keep them closed for several moments. Then do this process again. You may repeat the fixed-eye stare/closed-eye process two to five times. Notice how much deeper your experience of relaxation becomes with each time you close your eyes.

Once you close your eyes, focus your attention completely on your breathing. Be aware of when you breathe in and notice when you breathe out. The repetition will help you go deeper. Then after about a minute or so, open your eyes and focus again on the same spot straight ahead. Stay focused for a moment or so and then close your eyes again. Repeat this several times. Then begin your goal technique.

### *An Alternate Beginning for a Deeper Trance*

The following alternate technique may offer a deeper experience right from the beginning. It is also helpful for occasions when your mind is more active and you are having difficulty settling down and concentrating on one thing.

Begin with a fixed stare at one spot on the wall or ceiling. Notice and name three things you see with your peripheral vision. Then name three things you hear. Then state three things you feel. Begin again with things you see, continue with what you hear, and then with what you feel. You may do this out loud or silently to yourself. Do this over and over again until you feel that your eyes want to close. It will sound like this:

"I see the light fixture, I see the window, I see the bookshelf. I hear the sound of the fan, I hear my breathing, I hear a dog barking outside. I feel my feet in my shoes, I feel my hands touching my thighs, I feel my body relaxing." Then repeat the entire process. (You may repeat something over again. i.e. I see the window, I see the bookshelf, I see the window. Just be sure to repeat the process until your eyes want to close.) Do not judge your success according to your subjective experience. Some trance experiences feel profoundly relaxing. Others may be only mildly relaxing.

Yet each experience offers your mind/body an opportunity for deeper rest than actual sleep. You will more than likely notice a difference afterward. To leave this state, simply remind yourself to get re-acclimated to the room you are in and then open your eyes.

## *Techniques While in Hypnosis*

### *Goals*

Picture a colorful hot air balloon. Imagine putting a problem in the balloon. Then release the balloon and watch it go up into the sky until you can't see it anymore. This technique will help you let go of a problem you've been ruminating about. Your unconscious mind gets the problem to solve. This technique is also good for open-ended questions. For example, "What would be the best step to take with toward my fitness goals?"

### *End-Result Imagery*

You may want to use end-result imagery to imagine yourself leaving food on the plate or passing up some dessert. In these cases you would imagine things the way you want them to be. You would picture yourself feeling satisfied after your meal. You might see yourself waving off the offer of the pie.

Judy used this technique to first imagine herself feeling content having smaller portions of dessert. In the past, she had felt compelled to order a large ice cream cone. She'd often go back for a second. Now she pictured asking for a small one. She did the imagery for about a week or so. One day her children asked if she'd take them to the ice cream shop. Without giving much thought to her efforts to cut down, she surprised herself when she automatically ordered the smallest portion available. "It felt quite natural, not forced," she said. "It felt as if I'd always eaten the smaller size." After that incident, she continued with the end-result imagery. She got to the point where she would often eat only a bite or two of her children's ice cream and feel completely content without the need to order some for herself.

### *Sitting Waiting*

You can also use the trance state to ask for a solution to a problem from your higher self. One way to facilitate this is a technique called sitting waiting.

To begin the sitting waiting process, picture a hot air balloon. Create it as vividly as you can. Imagine the colors and size of the balloon, etc. The balloon is a vehicle to be used as a communication device between your consciousness and your higher self or wisdom self. Think of a problem you need help with. Now, put the problem in the balloon. You can use a symbol to represent the problem or even spell out the problem in a sentence. Imagine writing it in the air with chalk or a puff of smoke. See yourself put it in the balloon.

Now release the balloon and watch it rise above the tallest trees and beyond the clouds. When it is far enough up in the sky that you can no longer see it, notice how you feel. You may experience a release of the problem. You have given the problem to your higher self.

Now you wait for an answer. The answer may come in different forms. You may notice you have a different view of the problem and a different line of thinking. You may discover an opportunity avails itself to you, one which you wouldn't have perceived before you did this technique.

### *A Note About Paraliminal Tapes (See page 198)*

These unique audiotapes are designed for whole brain learning. You will hear one voice in one ear speaking to one part of your brain, while another voice in the other ear speaks to a different part of the brain. Very unusual, very pleasurable, and very effective.

No "questionable" subliminal messages are involved. You will find no short-term motivational hype. You will not hear fluffy affirmations or wishful positive statements. Rather, you will hear Paul Scheele, co-founder of Learning Strategies Corporation, skillfully guide your mind so that you get the results you want. To improve your life, sometimes all it takes is guidance to evoke your inner wisdom.

Paraliminal tapes increase your personal power by activating your "whole mind" with a precise blend of music and words. Each tape is carefully scripted to give you the best tape for your investment.

With paraliminal learning sessions, the listener can hear separate messages coming into each ear, but it is beyond the conscious mind's ability to process both messages simultaneously for more than a few moments. The result is an interesting multi-level communication to different hemispheres of the brain. The listener can choose which ear's information to attend to, and ones' attention tends to switch from time to time. Consequently, the conscious mind's experience of the tape is different with each listening session. Yet, the other-than-conscious (referred to as the "paraconscious" by Lozanov, 1978) receives the entire message each time.

Remember the quiz you took at the start of this book? This would be a good time to take it again. It's also a good time to re-examine the diagrams in the beginning of the book. Which of your attitudes and behaviors have begun to change already?

Picture your life one year from now. Imagine yourself the way you want to be. Each night as your head hits the pillow, make it a habit to take a minute to picture your continued progress. Make the image vivid and in color. This will assure your "other-than-conscious-mind" to work towards success.

**Good Luck! Keep on keeping on!**

# Resources

*Body Image: A Reality Check,* by Pamela Shires Sneddon

Although this is written for teens, any adult will benefit. There are a variety of healthy ways to perceive your body. By the time you are through reading, you will have a "body image make-over."

*Breaking Free from Compulsive Eating,* by Geneen Roth

Addresses the issue of compulsive eating and how to put an end to the anguish.

*The Dieter's Dilemma,* by William Bennett & Joel Gurin

A theory which will help you understand your limitations. You'll take a breath of relief when you realize you can stop trying to fit your size ten foot into a size five shoe.

*Feeding the Hungry Heart: The Experience of Compulsive Eating,* by Geneen Roth

Addresses the issue of compulsive eating and how to put an end to the anguish.

*Great Shape: The First Fitness Guide for Large Women*, by Pat Lyons & Debby Burgard

This book is an excellent resource for healthful living. It teaches exercise for every body shape: from the fit to the wanting to be fit.

*Intuitive Eating: A Recovery Book for the Chronic Dieter: Rediscover the Pleasures of Eating and Rebuild Your Body Image*, by Evelyn Tribole & Elyse Resch

Expand on the eating techniques that will save your soul. This book offers techniques as an adjunct to those in "Success for the Diet Dropout."

*Overcoming Overeating*, by Jane Hirschmann

A book to help you break out of the diet/binge cycle. Good food/bad food. Punishment/reward. These are the compulsive eater's nightmares, a long-time pattern of recrimination and guilt that ultimately leads to more overeating and more weight gain.

*Thin Is Just a Four-Letter Word: Living Fit for All Shapes and Sizes*, by Dee Hakala & Michael D'Orso

The story of one woman who had the courage to carve her own path to good body image.

*When You Eat At The Refrigerator, Pull Up A Chair: 50 Ways To Be Thin, Gorgeous, And Happy When You Feel Anything But*, by Geneen Roth, Anne Lamott

Addresses the issue of compulsive eating and how to put an end to the anguish.

*Your Fat Is Not Your Fault: Overcome Your Body's Resistance to Permanent Weight Loss*, by Margaret West, Carol N. Simontacchi & Barry Sears.

This is the most sensible approach to food I have ever read. It offers such a variety of eating styles, you are sure to find something that fits yours.

### *Organizations*

**Women Insisting on Natural Shapes (WINS)**
Founder: Dr. Ann Gerhardt 1-800-600-9467

**New Face of Fitness**
Founder: Dee Hakala www.deehakala.com

*Weight a Minute* on line newsletter. This newsletter addresses many issues including: "Can You Be Fit And Large?" and "How To Stay Motivated." It's free. Subscribe at: http://www.oxygen.com/newsletters/

# About the Author

Nikki Goldman, Ph.D., National speaker, award-winning writer, and therapist. Her weekly column, "Ask Dr. Nikki" appears in multiple California newspapers. She has written for national magazines, such as *Family Circle* and *BBW Magazine*. Her award-winning books are educational tools in schools across the nation. She has lectured at such renowned institutions as the University of California Medical School, and the United States Navy and is a frequent guest on radio talk shows. She uses hypnosis in her private practice to help people effect change by showing them how to use the power of their own mind. She lives with her husband, Gene, and their two girls, Shanna and Jessie, in Poway, California.

*Special Paraliminal Audiotapes*

**brought to you**

**courtesy of**

# Nikki Goldman, Ph.D.

## *Ideal Weight - $24.95*

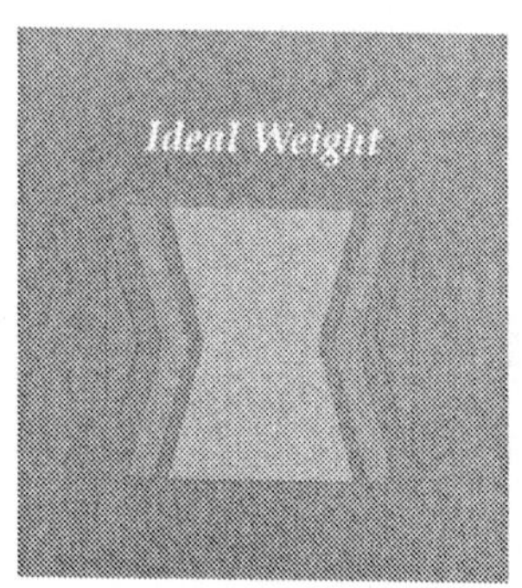


Your body signals you when to start eating, when to when to stop, and which foods to eat. This tape helps you discover and follow your natural signals. Say good-bye to roller coaster dieting forever with this remarkable tool.

Listen 20 minutes a day for 8 days. Then listen weekly until you have reached your ideal weight. Once you reach your ideal weight, you will maintain it naturally as you enjoy an optimal balance in your diet.

## *Self-Esteem Supercharger - $14.95*

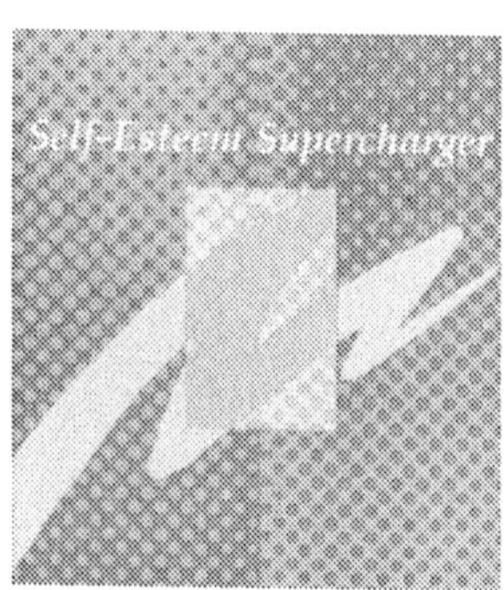


Face life challenges with a stronger belief in yourself. Improve willpower, determination, and stamina. Build confidence and self-assuredness. Feel better about yourself.

This tape helps remove negative influences of other people, situations, and your own self-talk. Listen to this tape to discover pleasant feelings of peacefulness and impending success. You can accomplish anything with the proper use of your mind. Customers say that this tape helps make all the others work better!

# Reinforce the Ideas in *Success for the Diet Dropout!*

***New Behavior Generator - $34.95***

Behaviors are at the root of everything we do. Use this tape to neutralize behaviors that hinder you and acquire new behaviors you want.

This is the most popular Paraliminal Tape, because it has unlimited uses. You are asked questions at the beginning of the tape about your goal and behaviors. Answer them to the best of your ability, lie back, relax, and generate behaviors you desire.

Shipping is just $4 for the first tape and $1 for each additional tape. Use Dr. Nikki's customer code to receive your discount:

***Code #DrNikki601***

PLUS, order both the New Behavior Generator and Ideal Weight, and receive a $14.95 discount.

To Order, go to:
www.DrNikkiGoldman.com
Click on the link to Learning Strategies
or call toll-free
1-866-DR-NIKKI
(1-866-376-4554)

# Quick Order Form

| | | |
|---|---|---|
| Telephone: | Call toll-free | 866-DrNikki |
| | | 866-376-4554 |
| | *Please have your credit card number ready* | |

e-mail Please submit to
DrNikki@DrNikkiGoldman.com

Postal: Please mail form to:
Behvioral Consultants Press
15708 Pomerado Rd., Ste. 201
Poway, CA 92064

Please send *Success for the Diet Dropout* to the address listed below. I understand that I may return this book for a full refund within 30 days, for any reason, no questions asked.

| | |
|---|---|
| ***Success for the Diet Dropout*** | $14.95 |
| Shipping and handling | 3.95 |
| California residents add 7.75% salex tax | 1.15 |

Name_______________________________________________

Address_____________________________________________

City, State__________________________________ zip________

*International shipping costs based upon actual cost to destination.*

Payment: ❑ check ❑ money order
credit card ❑ Visa ❑ MasterCard ❑ Discover

Card number__________________________________exp___ /___

Name on card_________________________________________

*Please order one book perfrom. You may reproduce this form as many times as desired.*

Printed in the United States
958900002B